Empty Force

Born in China, **Paul Dong** is an internationally known writer in the field of paranormal phenomena. He has taught chi kung for many years and is a master of the empty force art he describes in this book. He lives with his wife and family in California.

**Thomas Raffill** has studied with Paul Dong since 1987 and is a committed chi kung practitioner. A researcher, translator and consultant in international affairs, he has traveled extensively in China, Japan and Russia.

# Empty Force

THE ULTIMATE MARTIAL ART
THE POWER OF CHI FOR SELF-DEFENCE
AND ENERGY HEALING

## Paul Dong and Thomas Raffill

## ELEMENT

Shaftesbury, Dorset • Rockport, Massachusetts
Melbourne, Victoria

First published in Great Britain in 1996 by
Element Books Limited
Shaftesbury, Dorset SP7 8BP

Published in the USA in 1996 by
Element Books, Inc.
PO Box 830, Rockport, MA 01966

Published in Australia in 1996 by
Element Books and distributed by
Penguin Australia Limited
487 Maroondah Highway, Ringwood, Victoria 3134

Reprinted September 1996
Reprinted 1997

Cover illustration by Mark Tophan
Cover design by Bridgewater Books
Page design by Roger Lightfoot

Typeset by Footnote Graphics, Warminster, Wilts
Printed and bound in the USA by
Courier Westford, Inc.

British Library Cataloguing in Publication
data available

Library of Congress Cataloging in Publication
data available

ISBN 1–85230–783–8

## other titles by Paul Dong

*The Four Major Mysteries of Mainland China*
*Questions and Answers on the Subject of UFOs*
*Chi Gong: An Ancient Chinese Way to Health*

# Contents

# Acknowledgments

The authors would like to express their great appreciation to the contributors in Chapter 8 for their time and effort in sharing their ideas and experiences. We would especially like to thank tai chi and intention fist teacher Master Gregory Fong, President William Gough of the Foundation for Mind-Being Research, and Professor Deborah Woo of the University of California, Santa Cruz. All three did a great deal of work and wrote long, excellent articles for the section. Sadly, space did not allow us to include them in their entirety.

We would also like to thank the other contributors: Karen Cameron, James Coats, William Chun, Jane Hallander, Elliot Harvey, Steven Matias, Richard Mooney, Rosa Mui, and Jerry Pool. They have all been most generous in sharing their articles for this book.

We have also received the help and encouragement of many friends as we wrote this book, and it would be impossible to mention them all in the limited space available. For those who are not mentioned here, we hope you will still understand our sincere gratitude.

# Preface

Some Background for Both Skeptics and Over-believers

Can a person knock down another person without physical contact?

This question is more complicated than it seems. Many Westerners would dismiss the idea as some sort of magic trick or illusion. As a Westerner myself, I can say this reaction is a natural result of our ignorance and the biases of our culture.

Why not take a look at all the available information before forming a judgement?

In the Chinese cultural context, this is not a flashy trick, but a reflection of a deep principle of life. Chinese philosophy teaches us that the strongest power comes from harmony with, and non-resistance to, the flow of nature. It can be thought of as a kind of "empty force."

I do not like the image of a superbeing who takes on all comers by waving invisible power beams from the hands. One who thinks in this way has not learned self-control and will probably soon run out of power. It would be more realistic to keep in mind the special sources of the power, usually involving years of patient cultivation.

The Chinese call the power behind the empty force *chi*, the vital energy used in their health practice known as *chi kung* (also spelled *qi gong* or *chi gong*). The techniques of this practice are deceptively simple. The crucial step is meditation to relax the body and clear the mind of distractions. In this way, the power comes from nothing, or so it seems.

However, the greatest challenge is to master one's own mind

and spirit; and this is far more difficult to learn than mere physical techniques such as those of conventional martial arts. For the most fascinating element of this "power of nothing" is that it becomes a physical force which can affect others – the most dramatic illustration of the philosophy of achieving harmony with nature through non-resistance.

There was a brief display of a similar martial arts technique on the 1993 U.S. public television series "The Mind and Healing," hosted by the well-known journalist Bill Moyers (a former press secretary to U.S. President Lyndon Johnson). The episode showed an American martial arts student trying to assail his Chinese master. The master didn't make a move, but the student couldn't make the slightest attack on him.

This is probably the most difficult thing to believe for people unfamiliar with Chinese culture (indeed, even many Chinese find it hard to believe). How could intangible spiritual power overcome brute force? Western philosophy tends to divide the physical from the spiritual, while the Chinese approach considers that both are part of the same larger reality.

In the last few years traditional Chinese medical methods, such as acupuncture, herbalism and chi kung have gained more and more acceptance internationally. Reports are appearing in prestigious medical journals, international conferences are beginning to make serious examinations of these ancient systems of knowledge, while many places around the world now have official programs of certification for practitioners of Chinese medicine.

The use of chi kung for healing is an example of the physical effectiveness of the "power of nothing." The martial arts application of the empty force, of course, has never been seriously considered in Western-style science. But medical researchers are constantly discovering new things about the way the mind and body interact.

Thus, it is possible to attempt an explanation of the empty force which is more compatible with Western philosophical traditions. Western science recognizes that the meditation state does induce some purely physical effects, such as changes in brain wave patterns. And this may have stronger implications than people realize. For example, in its 7 March 1995 issue, the "Science Times" section of the *New York Times* carried an article entitled "How Brain Waves Can Fly a Plane," describing some research in which a person was trained to use brain waves to control an electrical device. Also, as mentioned above, many scientists and doctors are using modern techniques to study the Chinese traditional claims of strengthening the energy known as chi by meditation. But we should remember that the ancient Chinese had their own scientific methods and principles, and these claims about chi are backed by over two thousand years of their own medical investigation.

Although I am not myself a martial arts practitioner, I would like to take the opportunity to say that I am convinced of the health benefits of chi kung. I once had a most impressive demonstration of this when I accidentally caught my leg in a car door. Severe bruises covered most of my lower leg, and there was not much improvement for a week. Then I attended a banquet for a chi kung master with Paul Dong. Most of the attendants were chi kung students or friends of the master. I did not tell anyone of my bruised leg, but Paul asked the master to send his chi at my head "to stimulate my mind." To my great surprise, by the next day my bruises had almost disappeared.

In this book, we do not wish to present the empty force only as a spiritual belief. Nor do we attempt to offer a conclusive proof of its scientific validity. Our intention is simply to present the background, traditions and techniques of this practice and to point out some major issues for further debate and research. The rest is up to the reader's own judgement – and, possibly, personal experience through practice. Incidentally, since this book – though co-authored – is principally drawn from the words of the master, Paul Dong, the first person singular is used throughout.

Now, imagine a scene in which a bunch of heavyweight thugs are about to beat up a frail-looking empty force master. The martial arts fans among the readers will say, "Zap-pow! Knock them down!" The skeptics will say, "At least the master will be in spiritual balance while getting flattened." But neither of them speaks the whole truth. The authors hope this book will provide a fresh perspective and contribute to the dialogue in the fields of mind-body research and martial arts.

Thomas Raffill

Chapter One

# The Mystery of Chi

Chi is central to the idea of the empty force, although you may well not have heard of anything in the world as strange as this concept. When translators from other countries are faced with translating the commonly-used Chinese word chi, they are stuck. They worry that their translations may not convey the meaning or may be totally wrong. This is because the word chi has a wide variety of meanings in Chinese. There are all kinds of strange usages besides the normal meanings of "air" and "energy." Looking in a large Chinese dictionary, one finds 85 meanings listed for chi and, besides these, there are many peculiar conversational phrases not listed. Unless you were educated in China, you would have difficulty understanding the many sides of chi. For example, there are many common expressions such as *zheng chi* (honest dealing), *chi zhi* (temperament), *hao chi* (generous spirit), *ao chi* (arrogance), *hao ran zhi chi* (elevation of mind), *yuan chi* (primary matter), and *zhen chi* (true chi). There is a saying: "Three inches of chi (life breath) can be used in a thousand ways, but when death comes, it's all over." The "three inches of chi" here means yuan chi (primary matter). Chinese people believe that yuan chi exists at one's birth and is stored in the *dan tian* (below the navel at a distance measured by three finger widths). This is the location and source of the body's power.

The Chinese also believe that yuan chi must be combined with *tian chi* (Heaven chi), *di chi* (earth chi) and *ying chi* (nourishment chi, the chi derived from food and water) to form zhen chi (true chi). The movement of zhen chi in the body controls all of life's

1

activities and is connected with Heaven, earth and everything in the world (for example, trees, rivers, mountains, mists, rain, and so on), forming a complex of "Heaven and man." For this reason, a person's chi (seen here as energy or something more mysterious and still unknown) can be transmitted to another person or even to an object. This transference has two aspects – with or without physical contact. Thus a Chinese chi kung master with external chi (inner chi sent outward) can, without physical contact – as if by thought – heal a sick person or knock a person down with a sudden burst of chi. However strange this seems to non-Chinese, it is the mystery of chi.

Even for myself, a Chinese who grew up in China, it took me until the age of 16 to first see the mystery of chi with my own eyes. Because it was the first time I had seen something mysterious, I can still remember it as if it were yesterday, even though it happened many years ago. It was an autumn evening, and a crowd of villagers had formed around a street performer demonstrating the use of chi for healing. As I watched him move chi in his fingers (I didn't know then what I know now – that he was using his middle and index fingers in a form known as *jian zhi* or "sword finger" in the martial arts world), his gaze was firmly fixed on some acupuncture point of the patient, who was at a distance of about three feet. In moments, the patient cried out that it was too hot. Several more people tried it, all with similar results.

Without going into the issue of whether or not he cured the patients, I'd like to focus on this question: without physical contact, how did he make them so hot that they yelled? This is one reason why I later became interested in chi kung. As I now know, his chi came directly from his fingers and eyes, but not everyone can call up chi at will. It took many years of chi kung practice before he could achieve this. His power is called *ge kong dian xue*, "touching acupuncture points through the air".

Chi kung has three thousand years of history in China. It is an internal exercise (or mind exercise), and it has a remarkable effect on health. Chi kung practice can help prevent and cure diseases, prolong life, and increase strength and power for martial arts. Since it was popularized in China in 1979, medical experts from many countries have come to China to learn and do research about chi kung.

Currently, China classifies chi kung into sports chi kung, medical chi kung, and martial arts chi kung. The first of these has brought China many gold medals in international competitions. The second is more important: the use of chi kung for healing has saved the country a lot of money. Over time, the practice of chi kung leads to external chi (chi sent out of the body), and this can be used to provide energy healing for other people. Patients with intractable diseases can achieve better results by combining a self-healing practice of chi kung with external chi from a chi kung master. In recent years, the Chinese have combined external chi with acupuncture, achieving even greater success. As for martial arts chi kung – the subject of this book – anyone who practices martial arts will have greater power by practicing chi kung first. A fighter who has mastered it can endure longer than one using martial arts alone to resist an opponent.

## "MOVING THE HANDS IN CIRCLES"

Even more amazing things can be achieved by activating the body's latent potential through chi kung, such as sudden bursts of energy or a strengthening of the human magnetic field. I can give a very good example of the latter phenomenon. Ma Jiannan (James Ma) is a professor of chemistry at Hong Kong's Chinese University. He is the director of that university's Engineering Institute. He has also been director of the nuclear-magnetic resonance laboratory for many years. He once had hepatitis, but someone taught him a simple chi kung exercise: moving the hands in circles in front of the stomach every morning. He said he would usually feel something in his hands, numbness or shaking, after exercising for 15 minutes. Eventually there was some improvement in his health, and some strange things happened. One day, while he was moving his hands in circles, his pet wolfhound was running around him as usual. Without thinking, he waved his hand at his dog. To his surprise, the wolfhound collapsed instantly. After that, he discovered that moving the hands in circles creates a magnetic resonance effect. He often tested the effect on different animals of moving his hands in circles, and each time there was an unusual reaction.

When he told the secret of his hand-circling technique to his friends, they were very surprised. Because of this, they called it the "James Method." In an article called "The Working Principle of Chi Gong – Magnetic Resonance" which he submitted to the 12th volume of the Chinese magazine *Chi Gong and Science* in 1988, he pointed out that as we practice moving our hands in circles in front of our stomachs, we are moving the blood in the hands, the red blood cells in the blood, and the magnetic material in the red blood cells across the earth's magnetic lines of force, thus creating a direct current and a magnetic field. Not only that, but if we provide the right frequency, we can cause the water in the hands to undergo nuclear-magnetic resonance. Magnetic resonance comes through the media of water and organic compounds and flows through the body. The direction of the flow can be guided by the hands, because the palms give off a rather strong magnetic resonance during this practice. It also may flow from the point of highest energy to the point of lowest energy. If the energy flows through damaged, weak, sick or old organs, they will be restored. This explains not only the connections between the magnetic fields of the body, magnetic resonance in the body, and the mystery of chi, but also some principles of chi kung's healing power.

I do not know Dr. Ma, but in my twenty years of teaching the empty force, energy healing chi kung, and yin and yang eight diagram chi kung (the most powerful group-healing chi kung, using two males and two females), I have always put "moving the hands in circles" first. However, I call it "push hands" (see pp. 76–7). Independently of Dr. Ma, I long ago discovered that this exercise could produce very strong energy and magnetism, which greatly helps in using external chi for healing.

Dr. Ma is well-known in the Hong Kong scientific community and in chi kung research circles. In 1987, he spent 100,000 Hong Kong dollars (about $12,500 or £8,300) to go to the South Pole for a chi kung experiment which lasted only 56 hours. He wanted to test the effects on the human body of the magnetic field on the ocean floor at the South Pole. He did the chi kung exercise of moving hands in circles on the ocean floor at 54.5 degrees South latitude, and discovered that the feeling of chi was particularly strong there. He also learned that the Antarctic Ocean waves have very high infrasonic energy, far greater than the combined infrasonic energy of millions of chi kung masters.

(You might also be interested to know that Dr. Ma made his trip on the only steamboat licensed to carry passengers from Chile across the Magellan Straits. He was the first Chinese passenger on this boat as well as the first person to dive under a yet-unnamed glacier, so the captain of the boat decided to call it "James Ma Glacier" – a name used on world maps ever since!)

Based on the results of his years of research, Dr. Ma published a paper at the First International Symposium on Acupuncture, Beijing 1987, called "Explaining Chinese Chi Gong by Magnetic-Nuclear Resonance" – "an initial hypothesis" he stated, "awaiting experimental evidence or correction of its mistakes by the world's researchers." Later, in the summer of 1992, Dr. Ma passed through California on his way to Canada. Here, Dr. Kenneth M. Sancier, director of the East-West Academy of Healing Arts, invited him to the city of Menlo Park to give a talk on chi kung to familiarize Californians with his theories.

## CHI AND SCIENCE

Infrasonic sound, mentioned above, may be related to some of the injury-producing effects of the empty force. As we know, infrasound is vibration at a very low frequency, inaudible to the human ear; and, although its energy is also very low, some infrasound can injure a person's internal organs, sometimes fatally. To my knowledge, effects of external chi which have been measured by instruments in China include infrasound, low-frequency amplitude-modulated infrared radiation, low-frequency magnetic information, particle flow information, visible or super-faint light, and organic ion flow, among others. Since the external chi "sent out instantaneously" by a chi kung master includes infrasound, this may account for the empty force's potential for damage.

There is a reason for using the term "sent out instantaneously": when a chi kung master is hit by a surprise attack and responds instantly, the chi he sends out is stronger; such powerful chi is permeated with infrasound. In contrast, when a chi kung master gives an external chi healing, the chi is moderate and is unlikely to have an infrasound component, if only because there has never been a reported case of a patient being injured by external chi treatment. External chi comes from the fingers and palm, guided by moderate intention, and enters the body. It has only good effects on the body.

Chinese scientists studying chi kung point out that infrasound effects come primarily from wave motion and undulation, not energy. For example, in the healing effects of the infrared heat radiation in external chi, it is not its energy, but its wave motion and undulation which can produce physiological changes and medical benefits. Tests with measuring instruments show that infrared radiation from the palms and fingers of a non-practitioner of chi kung does not have the same coherent wave motion and undulation, and so does not produce any noticeable effects. Before such measurements had been made, some people believed that external chi worked like an "electric toaster" in physiotherapy, producing effects merely by exposing the injured spot to infrared heat radiation. That this is not the case is shown by the results of repeated experiments: the infrared heat radiation in external chi has a power level of only a few tenths of a microwatt ($\mu$W), while that of medical infrared heat radiators on the market is a few tenths of a kilowatt (kW). A microwatt ($10^{-6}$ W) and a kilowatt ($10^3$ W) are several orders of magnitude apart. The infrared heat radiation given off by a chi kung master, although extremely faint, has much stronger healing effects than the infrared heat radiation of physiotherapy, which is hundreds of millions of times higher in energy. This indicates that the energy level is not a major factor in external chi's efficacy.

Nor does energy level play a role when a chi kung master instantly sends chi to injure an attacker. The wave motion and undulation are the important things. What *is* the reason behind the empty force's ability to knock down or push back an opponent? According to a paper on "The Material Basis and Physical Effects of External Chi" by Professor Xie Huanzhang of the Beijing Institute of Industrial Science, the wave motion and undulation carries information, and the organism of a master in the chi kung state is sufficiently sensitive to respond to it, or resonate with it. This produces the effect on the target of being knocked down or pushed back. If we focus our attention on Dr. Ma's "moving the hands in circles" effect, Prof. Xie Huanzhang's "information" effect, and the "wave motion and undulation" effect pointed out by the Chinese scientists, we will come to realize that the empty force is not "empty." There is some reason for its ability to knock people down or injure them.

In the past decade, China has put a great deal of manpower and material into chi kung research. This is because Chinese scientists encourage the government to conduct such research, not only because of the contribution of chi kung can make to health

*Figure 1   Master Yu Yongnian (left) guiding students in "moving the hands in circles" at a chi kung conference*

and medicine, but also for some surprising applications both to the military and to agriculture (don't forget: China is primarily an agricultural country).

In the former case, it enhances the ability and health of soldiers (not to mention the advantage of having people with psychic powers serving the national defense!) In the latter, Wu Shengshen of the Chinese Academy of Science Changchun Physics Institute, for example, describes in his article "External Chi Material and its Effects on Growth and Death" how in 1981 the Chinese Academy of Science in Shanghai used all kinds of instruments to measure the microwaves in external chi (3mm, 5mm and 8mm wave bands), the infrared band and blue-green visible light (420mm wave band). These experiments were conducted behind a screen of lead containers on the assumption that chi kung cannot go through lead walls; but that turned out to be wrong. Later, in 1986, experiments in Changchun showed that external chi is a substance with strong directionality and fine bore, which enables it to penetrate lead plates. It also turned out that some external chi can give off gamma ray wave bands.

*Figure 2   Chinese "super psychic" Yan Xin pictured during his visit to the U.S.A., at a welcoming party in San Francisco*

Thus, in August 1987, a national chi kung technical conference in China enthusiastically discussed the issue of gamma ray penetration of lead walls. From September 1987 to September 1988, three research teams investigated this anomaly which was arousing such excitement. Cooperating with chi kung master Yan Xin (known as "China's super psychic") and the Beijing High Energy Physics Institute, they found high-energy particles of gamma rays and neutrons in external chi. On another occasion, working with "one-finger art" chi kung master Liu Zonglin and Xi'an Communications University, they performed three experiments, including one which determined that external chi contains gamma rays. Later, they tested external chi passing through a two-centimeter thick lead board (ten times thicker than the one used in the 1986 tests in Changchun). In a further experiment, Shandong Medical College Associate Professor Jing Ziliang and Changchun Physics Institute's Wu Wei cooperated in testing the sending and receiving of external chi at long distances. They also detected the presence of gamma radiation.

The importance of gamma rays in external chi lies in its ability to destroy cancer cells both on the surface of and within the body. Its energy is higher than that of X-rays. China had already used external chi to treat cancer and there was nothing new about this. China's research on gamma rays indicates that there is a difference between the effects of high doses and low doses of gamma rays. At the proper dosage, it not only does no harm, but is even beneficial to growth. Professor Wang Jialin from Sichuan Province imported a species of mushroom from Japan, and the largest one grew to 2.52 kilograms after external chi treatment. The productivity rate was raised by 34 percent, and the time of growth was speeded up by 31.5 percent. The Japanese were very impressed! In the light of these experiments, we begin to wonder whether the skeptics shouldn't consider afresh the ability of the empty force to knock down or injure an opponent or "target" without physical contact.

## THE PSYCHIC POWER OF CHI

Any discussion of the mystery of chi must include mention of psychic phenomena. Perhaps these occur on an even higher level than chi – the whole question awaits further research. However, I would like to describe a very interesting personal experience – directly connected with chi – which I found unforgettable.

On a trip to Mainland China in October 1990, I made an appointment with Yao Wenjiang, a high-level engineer at the Research Institute of Bohai Oil Corporation, to meet him in his home, because he has a daughter with many psychic powers. I brought with me three editors from the *Journal of UFO Research* (published in Gansu Province, China; circulation 320,000), to see some demonstrations of her abilities and also to do some tests on whether chi might be related to psychic ability.

This young girl is named Yao Zheng. At the age of 16, she studied in Dagu Middle School in Tianjin. One day, during an examination, a schoolmate suddenly saw smoke rising from Yao Zheng's back and two holes burned in her clothes (one would logically expect her to feel pain from the burning before it reached this stage), and people were thrown into panic. The teacher was staring speechlessly, and nobody could do anything to help until the fire burned through the two holes. This is a typical event: she often loses control of herself and burns articles of her clothing such as shoes, socks, skirts, handkerchiefs, etc. Her parents are terribly afraid of her "spirit fire," and once asked for help from a Professor Song (the information source may have changed the name) of the Chinese Institute for Space Medicine. His opinion was that few people carried such quantities of static electricity on the body, but there had been cases of it in psychics around the world. But the ability of Yao Zheng to burn paper with the palm of her hand and leave marks in the shape of pictures and words was a rare phenonemon, and should be carefully observed, recorded and studied. This is a new area of psychic research.

This task was handed over to the Chinese Defense Ministry, Nankai University, Institute for Space Medicine, and Health Ministry (I'm not sure why the Health Ministry got involved) for further study. But that is a matter for those research organizations. My main focus was to find out whether she would burn more fiercely if I added my chi to her psychic abilities. I asked her parents to let me test this. I told them I had a lot of chi, including healing chi (helping power), and empty force chi (fighting power). Her mother, Wang Lei, is a pediatrician. She replied: "We had no choice but to ask researchers to find a way to turn off her ability, because we are not just worried about her burning her own clothes, but more about burning other people. She has not been burning things for two months now, and we don't want her to start again."

For this reason, we had to give up on this experiment. But we did do three other experiments, including one which involved opening flowers, one which attempted to remove tablets from a sealed bottle, and one that tested telekinesis.

I picked several rosebuds from a flower garden in their village and gave them to Yao Zheng. She put the flowers on her palm, closed her hands around them, and lightly waved them by her ear. In about five minutes, she said the flowers had opened. When she did the flower-opening a second time, I raised my arms to send chi to her head. This time, the flower opened after only two minutes. One of the editors said that when I added chi to her, he saw her palms give off a violet light (but the other two editors didn't see it, maybe because they weren't paying attention). He also expressed a reservation: "We can't be sure that she didn't speed up the second time because she had already done it once, so how about trying it without adding chi next time?" We all thought that this made sense, so, following his suggestion, we devised a new test: removing tablets from a sealed bottle by mind power. This time she tried for ten minutes but the tablets

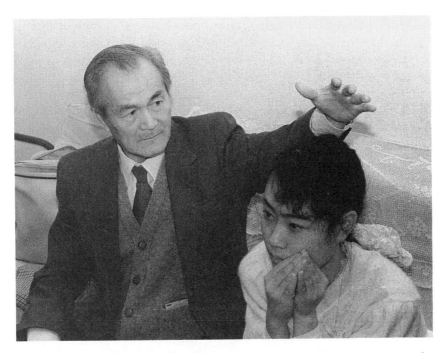

*Figure 3  This psychic lady, who demonstrates the power to make flower buds open with her mind, told Paul Dong that she could open the buds more easily when he sent the empty force power to her*

wouldn't come out, and she was getting tired of shaking the bottle in her hand. I saw that she couldn't do it without assistance, so I sent chi from my eyes to her hands, and not long afterwards, white pills came out from the bottom of the bottle. One of the pills was crushed. I wouldn't presume to judge whether it was a coincidence of timing of whether it was my chi. Afterwards, we again tried to remove the pills from the bottle without adding chi. This time, a bunch of black pills came out of the bottle in three minutes. Can chi kung's chi be combined with psychic chi to produce stronger effects?

The next day, we did two flower-opening tests. Whenever I added chi, the flower opened faster. Finally, we did a telekinesis experiment. I put a spoon on the table, and asked her to move it by psychic power alone. She lowered her head in meditation, adjusting her mind. But for 20 minutes, the spoon didn't move. Finally, I directed chi to her *yin tang* acupuncture point (between the eyes), and asked her to move the spoon with her mind. Right away, the spoon flew off the table. We couldn't find it for a while. (Chinese psychic researchers believe that this type of flight, which they call "unobservable flight," cannot be seen by anybody, no matter how fast or slow it is.) Later, her father found the spoon on a shelf, buried behind a pile of papers.

These little experiments are not enough to prove a connection between chi kung and psychic phenomena, and there is no reason not to view it as a coincidence, but I know there are many things going on in China in chi kung and psychic research, and I can't help but associate the two. However, since this book is about the empty force and not about psychic abilities, I shall not cite all the sources now. Here I'd just like to mention that my work in progress, *China's Super Psychics*, will be mostly about chi.

## MYSTERIOUS CHI

In my mind, chi is a package of mysteries, not something which can be explained in a word or two. This is as much a dilemma for me as for the non-Chinese translators. When we break a wooden club with one blow of the hand, the Chinese believe it is a combination of chi and force. The Chinese also speak of "having chi but no force" and "having force but no chi." The former refers to a person who has sufficient chi but has not trained the ribs, bones, skin and muscles, and is therefore physically weak and unable to take a hit, while the latter means one who is physically strong but doesn't have enough chi to support his or her strength and make use of it. One with real strength would be both physically and spiritually strong.

For this reason, one who exercises the ribs, bones, skin and muscles should exercise the chi at the same time. Exercising the chi is what the Taoists called the cultivation of *jing* (essence), chi, and *shen* (spirit), a kind of "internal exercise." (Note that this jing is not the same as the jing of *ling kong jing*, or empty force – see glossary.) This internal exercise will produce inner force, which can give rise to many strange things in combination with special powers and the mind – for example, healing power, psychic ability, or the empty force. The mystery of chi is a broad topic, and this chapter is only the beginning. For the Chinese, chi will always be mysterious.

# Chapter Two

# The Empty Force

Martial arts are of the greatest interest to men and women who want to learn self-defense for their own protection, to develop spiritual balance and self-mastery, or to learn the mysterious traditions of Oriental culture. No wonder this field has not lost its luster over thousands of years of development. Now it has spread beyond China and planted firm roots all over the world. Look in the phone book of any medium-sized or large city in America, Europe, or Australia and you will find martial arts schools. Film star Bruce Lee's millions of fans worldwide bear eloquent witness to its popularity.

Martial arts originated in ancient times as a means for health promotion and self-defense. Continuing to grow and develop up to the present, it now includes such sophisticated techniques as the iron pellet palm (see p. 21), the one-finger art (see p. 24), and the astonishing *ding shen fa* (a technique for paralysing a target with one touch – see p. 24). However, in one sense, these terrifying techniques are actually nothing special, because they all rely on physical contact for their effects. What I am revealing here for the first time is something completely different, a martial art technique called *ling kong jing*, which has come to be known in the United States as the "empty force". This term refers to a power which can strike a person through the air, without physical contact. A mild attack by this force will hurt the opponent or "target" (inducing hot and cold spells, vomiting, dizziness, or headaches), while a strong attack is even reputed to lead to death. If the target of the attack is sensitive to chi and attempts

*Figure 4   The invisible empty force from Paul Dong penetrates a line
of students at the San Francisco College of Acupuncture*

to resist the force, then he may be thrown back several feet or
even be sent flying through the air. But if the force is used for
healing, it can cure many chronic diseases.

Because China is renowned as a center for martial arts, many
novels on the subject have been written over the last three
thousand years. Many of these mention a powerful technique
called "thunder palm" where, at the point when an opponent is
at his most threatening, one lets out a great sound, as if from the
palm, which knocks down the opponent. As a child living in
China, I was unable to judge whether or not "thunder palm"
really existed, but I felt that if it did, it would be the greatest art
in the world and whoever knew it would be unbeatable.

Now I can say that there is no such thing as "thunder palm" in
the secret traditions of Chinese martial arts. However, there is
something similar, the empty force, which has the same charac-
teristic of knocking down an opponent without physical contact.
Indeed, perhaps the empty force was the model for the literary

invention of "thunder palm." The novelists may have used artistic license to exaggerate and embellish it by adding the sound (a clap of thunder) and conjuring up an image of the target being suddenly struck by lightning. In those imaginary scenes, not only is the target knocked down, but even the surrounding grass, trees and rocks are destroyed.

## THE FORCE THAT GOES THROUGH WALLS

It is hard to trace back the origins of the empty force, but we know that Yang Luchan (1799–1872) – a famous *tai chi chuan* expert in China's Qing Dynasty who was said to "draw blood with every step" – had mastered the empty force. For this reason, people say that the tradition of the empty force was lost and reappeared during the Qing Dynasty. It was claimed that whenever Yang's life was in danger, he would kill one assailant with every step. However, what he let out of his palm was not "thunder," but what the Chinese call "jing" (force). As soon as this force is sent out, nothing can block it except aluminum or a mirror. It has the power to penetrate not only wooden boards, but also walls, bricks and even iron.

An article by Dong Shiqi, published in 1989 in the Chinese-American newspaper *Zhong Bao*, describes a demonstration of the empty force in Hong Kong by the master Cai Songfang. He wrote:

> Several friends in a Chinese club gave a banquet for Mr. Cai Song-fang in a Chinese restaurant as a welcoming party for him. I was one of the guests. After the meal, I asked Master Cai to demonstrate the empty force in the spacious hall. Mr. Su was the first to agree to this and he stood about ten feet back. Master Cai raised his hand gently, and Mr. Su was pushed back 5 or 6 steps (remember, this was only a demonstration and the master was holding back to avoid injuring the target). The hall we were in had a cement pillar about a foot thick, so Master Cai asked another guest, Mr. Mai, to go behind the cement pillar and stand about four or five feet back. Master Cai then got on the other side of the pillar and lightly gestured with his hand, but Mr. Mai wasn't protected in the least by the intervening pillar. Just as Mr. Su did, he became unsteady on his feet and almost fell down.

I have done many experiments to determine whether the empty force can really penetrate walls, stone blocks, or any other

*Figure 5    Paul Dong sends the empty force through a wooden board at
a scientist's house for an experiment.*

intervening materials. On several occasions in 1991, I asked the
students in my chi kung class at the San Francisco College of
Acupuncture to stand behind the concrete-reinforced walls. They
can attest that my empty force went through the walls to their
bodies.

I looked everywhere for materials to prove the existence of the
empty force and its relationship to tai chi chuan, including
libraries, friends' book collections, etc. Finally, I found what I
was looking for. My friend John Lee gave me a book called *The
Book of Taiji Quan* [i.e. tai chi chuan – see glossary] which has a
description and definition of the empty force:

> The empty force is very mysterious, almost mystical, and has to be
> seen to be believed. It is a manifestation of the spirit. A high master
> of this art only has to let out a cry and the target will have his feet
> lifted off the ground and will be pushed back. This is probably
> because the one receiving the force is attracted by the one releasing
> the force and is unable to resist it . . . . It is said that long ago Yang
> Luchan and his son were able to attract the flame of a candle almost
> a foot away. At the move of a hand, the candle flame would gradu-
> ally go out. This was one of the techniques of the empty force, but its
> tradition has died out.

The tradition which "died out" here referred to the technique of "attracting a candle flame a foot away" and not the empty force as a whole. The empty force has followed an unbroken line from the alleged "thunder palms" to the "falling dragon palms" (which I shall discuss shortly); from Wang Xiangzhai's empty force, which caused a sensation in Northern China in the 1920s (see p. 27), right up to the present when the empty force is so controversial in the U.S. It has existed continuously among the Chinese people and has never died out, although it appears that – for certain periods – there was a gap in the historical record of its demonstration by masters. I would speculate that the gap can be attributed to the difficulty of attaining the empty force, which requires two to four hours of practice every day, 365 days a year, without a break. This has to be kept up for at least three to five years before the results will be apparent. Of course, the strength of the power depends on the length of practice.

Moreover, the most important condition is to maintain a peaceful and quiet state of mind. This is not possible for many people, especially those who live in the cities. For this reason, the empty force is usually learned by Taoist priests who live in the solitude of mountains, away from crowds.

When the Shanghai empty force master You Pengxi (1902–1983) came to the U.S. to teach the empty force in San Francisco, some said that it would be impossible to do so because the Americans' lifestyle is too busy, and they are unable to attain quietness of mind, surrounded as they are by images of movie stars, pop singers, ball games, money, cars, and sex. This is a valid criticism but, even so, it is possible to swim against this tide of commercialism and, through strict discipline, master the art: as we shall see in Chapter 4, You Pengxi's wife introduced me to two students who she said had very strong empty force power.

When in the preceding section I discussed "thunder palm" and the empty force, I also mentioned the "falling dragon palm" – and with reason. For there is a clue to the relationship between this, possibly fictional, technique and the empty force in the work of Jin Yong, a Hong Kong newspaper chief who also writes martial arts novels. His best-selling *The Eagle-Shooting Heroes* (1976) tells the story of five martial arts masters during China's Song Dynasty (960–1126). Each master had a special skill, and one of them, named Hong Qigong, was a master of "falling dragon palms," just as terrible as "thunder palms." Both skills involve a force transmitted through the palms of the hands. At the time of sending, "the left leg is slightly bent, the right arm is curved in, and the right palm draws three circles. Then, with a shout, they are extended outward." This is exactly the same as the action used to practice the empty force. Since Jin Yong is very knowledgeable, especially about the mysteries of ancient martial arts, he couldn't fail to have seen the similarity between the empty force and his description of "falling dragon palms." And so, it seems likely that they, together with "thunder palms," are one and the same thing.

## ENERGY HEALING

So far, I have only discussed the martial arts applications of the empty force, but it has more than one use. Besides self-defense, it can also be used as an aid to healing of sick people.

A kind of natural therapy which doesn't require medicines, injections, doctors, or money, energy healing can take the form of self-healing or of healing for others. In the latter case, the healer performs a sort of "acupuncture" by transmitting rich vital energies from his own internal body into the appropriate acupuncture point in the patient. Because this doesn't require needles or, indeed, any physical contact with the patient's body, there is no pain (acupuncture involves slight pain). Energy healing is usually most effective in the treatment of chronic diseases.

Such healing power is usually attained by doing Chinese chi kung exercises, which are generally based on meditation and, above all, on a crucial exercise called standing-on-stake (*zhan zhuang*), the movements of which will be described in detail in Chapter 7.

There is a type of chi kung, specifically designed for energy healing, which is called "healing chi kung." By practicing an hour a day, one can master it in nine months to one year. However, its energy is not as powerful as that of the empty force – which requires at least three years of practice, without meanwhile releasing any of the energy in order to allow it to build up. The most serious practitioners would wait five years before using the energy. Although it takes longer to learn than energy healing, it is many times stronger. Sometimes, for instance, one can use mind power alone to direct the energy to enter the patient's body, without needing to use the fingers or palms. This is similar to the ability of those born with psychic healing power. Both are related to chi kung.

## "STANDING-ON-STAKE"

In ancient times, anyone who wanted to learn martial arts had to learn chi kung first, in order to strengthen the body's internal energy. Only with rich internal energy can one attain powerful martial arts abilities, but because of the constant development of a more complex society, people have gradually become busier, and martial arts students, looking for a shortcut, have neglected chi kung. Gradually they came to abandon the principle: "to learn martial arts, first practice chi kung." Students of tai chi chuan also have the same failing. Originally, before starting to learn tai chi chuan one would have to practice standing-on-stake first, but being too busy or unwilling to put in the time for that, tai chi practitioners took a short-cut and abandoned standing-on-stake. Eventually, people didn't even remember the principle: "to learn tai chi chuan, first practice standing-on-stake." Since this sort of practice neglected the foundation, the results were far from ideal. The reason Yang Luchan could "draw blood with every step" was the power he gained from doing standing-on-stake. It is clear that his empty force was related to tai chi chuan, for tai chi, martial arts, and chi kung are three aspects of the same essential practice.

My teacher's master, Wang Xiangzhai (1886–1963), caused a sensation all over China because he had mastered the empty force. The "*yi quan*" (intention fist – a combination of martial arts and chi kung with an emphasis on mind power) he invented in the 1920s is based on standing-on-stake. Indeed, the convention to commemorate the 30th anniversary of his death, held in Beijing on 24 July 1993, declared that it is "the most basic method of practicing yi quan." We can go further and say that standing-on-stake is the highest principle – the greatest secret – of martial arts. Lao Tzu's words – "Stand alone without changing, to see the mystery; carry on fully, to see the limits" – can be interpreted as meaning: "Standing motionlessly [i.e. standing-on-stake] will later make you realize the mysteries, and persisting in it will eventually bring you benefits." The famous ancient Chinese medical encyclopedia *The Yellow Emperor's Classic of Internal Medicine* also says: "Stand alone quietly and preserve the spirit, and all parts of the body will be as one," which means that "standing in a quiet manner and concentrating will center the body." Standing-on-stake is therefore the key to centering the body's energy; and from this center, in turn, flows the empty force, a martial arts power we can hardly imagine today.

Chapter Three

# The Empty Force Masters

China is truly a wonderland of martial arts. Zhengzhou in Henan Province, China, is known as the "martial arts village." Shaolin Monastery (famous for "Shaolin martial arts," and used as the setting for David Carradine's hit TV series *Kung Fu*) is just one of its points of interest. Where I grew up, in Taishan County, there was another local martial arts village. In those days every village had its own martial arts instruction. The prosperous ones would hire famous martial arts masters locally or even from far away to come and teach. Less prosperous villages were only able to hire lesser masters.

## DEMON-FOOT, TIGER-CLAW, AND OTHER MASTERS

I spent the first 17 years of my life in Taishan County. I not only studied martial arts, I also heard many stories about it. For example, the most terrifying person we knew was a martial arts master from Beifen Village, a man called Huang Mingsheng. He was said to be able to kill a person with one blow. Not only that, he was also said to be able to cause severe injury to a horse or an ox with one blow. The art he practiced was "yin-yang palms," an even more powerful technique than "iron pellet palms," in which the fists are made to become as solid as iron, and one blow will be enough to "curdle the blood," leave a scar, or seriously injure the target. "Yin-yang palms," in contrast, does not "curdle the blood," but instead knocks out the target instantly as if by a powerful electric shock, irreparably damaging the internal organs.

Another well-known master in Taishan was called "Demon-Foot Master." He excelled in using the legs, with footwork as good as Bruce Lee's. Normally, a beginner in martial arts was supposed to practice the "horse-trot" (standing-on-stake) posture for three months, or six months at most. But students of "Demon-Foot Master" had to do the horse-trot for one year before he would begin to teach them martial arts. The impatient ones would usually give up in the middle, but those who did learn the demon-foot would become local heroes. Because the leg is longer than the arm and has more power, using it flexibly can be a decisive advantage. Martial arts superstar Bruce Lee had a deep understanding of this principle, and that is why he placed a high value on footwork. He beat his opponents by jumping and kicking at their upper bodies. In contrast, Demon-Foot Master concentrated on the lower body. He specialized in sweeping his legs around to trip up his opponents and make them fall. If he happened to be knocked down himself, he would immediately roll around and attack his opponent's legs. The opponent, still feeling the thrill of victory, would be unprepared to dodge and would take a beating. In the famous classical Chinese novels *The Three Kingdoms* and *Water Margin*, this trap was called "fallen horseman fighting."

I can't resist mentioning here one master whom I knew personally, "Tiger-Claw King." Unlike the Demon-Foot Master, he beat his opponents with his hands. He exercised his fingers to make them as tough as a tiger's claws, and would not only scratch the target's skin, causing bleeding and injury, but could also, it was said, go horrifyingly wild and tear a person's heart out of his chest, rip the intestines out of the stomach and shred the internal organs . . .

I saw him with my own eyes tear the bark off trees. He could easily rip through the tough bark of a pine tree. Tiger-Claw was particularly adept at fighting someone larger than himself, because anyone with huge, sprawling limbs would bleed profusely as soon as Tiger-Claw scratched through the skin.

He liked to drink soup derived from animal bones and to eat meat from animal muscles (any animal would do). The reason was that bones contain large amounts of calcium (there were no calcium tablets in the village in those days), and calcium helps strengthen the fingernails. Meat contains large amounts of collagenous material, and this helps toughen the muscles. Both were helpful to his "tiger claws." He would also drink rice wine – one glass with every dinner. In Chinese medicine it is believed that drinking a moderate amount of wine is good for the blood circulation. (Only in the last few years has Western medicine proven that wine can help the circulation and decrease the risk of heart disease.) Good circulation makes one's strength more effective.

One particularly remarkable habit of his was to trim his fingernails in his spare time every day. I can remember asking him why he did this, but he didn't answer me. Perhaps he was afraid I was too young and wouldn't understand (I was 14 at the time). I didn't press him for an answer, but later I heard that he had to keep his nails at just the right length. If he made them too long, they would break off too easily, but if he made them too short, he wouldn't be able to claw through people's skin.

I discovered another secret of his. He used something to protect the fingernails of his middle finger and ring finger. His reason was that these nails were a little longer than the others and were liable to be more easily damaged.

He taught his students to strengthen their fingers every day by scraping them in the dirt, scraping bits of metal, or even scraping the bark off trees. Amazingly, he himself would scrape the skin off bulls and horses, making the animals cry out – not, of course, a practice we would endorse. After doing the scraping exercise, he would massage his hands and soak them for 15 minutes in a hot water concoction containing many Chinese herbal medicines.

Those local masters, however, are as nothing compared to the top national masters. It is said that Li Denglai of Beijing police headquarters can "shatter a stone by spitting." He carries no guns or knives – the only thing in his holster is a bottle of water, all the weapon he needs. When he spits this water at an opponent, it is more effective than a gun or a knife, either of which, after all, can sometimes miss the mark; but Mr. Li's spray could never miss during a fight. For even if only one drop of water hits the target, it will slash open the skin just as an air gun might. There are only two ways to escape his attack: first, by not giving him a chance to put the water in his mouth, or second, by running away as fast as possible to avoid getting hit by a drop of water.

It is said that Li has practiced chi kung for 20 years and can split open a stone by spitting water at it – a feat which can be confirmed by the Beijing city government or police department, where Li has become something of a celebrity.

Ding shen fa (a technique for paralyzing someone with one touch) is another unique and overpowering Chinese art, which often appears in martial arts novels. One who has mastered it is revered as a "superior being." Only a few such masters are reputed to exist in all of China. During a battle, the decisive factor is whether or not you are touched by the master. If you are, you will be paralyzed instantly and the only thing you'll be able to move will be your mouth – to beg for mercy and admit defeat. If the master is not impressed by that, he might leave you there for a few hours or a day before coming back and releasing the point that was touched.

Everyone in the martial arts world knows of the "one-finger art" of the late priest Hai Deng of Shaolin Monastery (the teacher of "super-psychic" master Yan Xin). He was supposed to be able to make his finger as sharp as a knife that could cut through a human body or even a wooden board.

## THE EMPTY FORCE – A CLASS APART

China has other amazing and esoteric arts too numerous to mention in detail here. As the Chinese say, "For every strong person there's somebody stronger." And yet, all the arts described above, with the exception of "shattering a stone by spitting," require bodily contact to have any effect. In this respect, the empty force is in a class by itself. It can achieve powerful results without physical contact. Perhaps it is an effect based on the interaction between the magnetic fields of two people's bodies; or perhaps it is some form of static electricity. At any rate, I can personally confirm that when I practice chi kung, it feels like electricity, particularly in the skin. After one has practiced for five or six hours a day over several years, there is no doubt that the practitioner's body can produce larger amounts of energy which become available for use.

The wise people of ancient times may have attained enlightenment from sitting in meditation. In this regard, it was said that "stillness gives rise to wisdom." They discovered that the combination of thought and action, or the use of a sudden word (such as shouting "hey"), enabled one's internal energy to be directed outward toward others. Chinese chi kung has a saying: "Chi follows the mind." (Western practices like psychic healing and energy healing also work by mind power.) A careful observer will notice that any sudden movement (such as swaying the body or moving the hand) is accompanied by the sensation of an electric current – especially for one who is practicing martial arts. If during a fight we are alert to the use of sudden words – for instance, to a master's shout of "hey" – we are able to anticipate the heaviest blow. A successful shout will knock the opponent down as if by a kind of "linguistic shock." If one combines thought, sudden action and sudden words, the effect will be even stronger. It is precisely under these conditions that the internal energy is released. The empty force is difficult for people to understand, and it is hard to accept unless one has seen it with one's own eyes. The events described below may help the reader to understand its reality.

## A High-Level Healer

I have been lucky enough to meet a higher level master who can put out a fire with his chi. It was the thrill of a lifetime to see this uncanny art. It took a week of searching in three cities before I met Master Zhang. With an introduction from a friend, I went from Beijing to Shanghai to meet him; but he had already gone to Tianjin, so I had to cross the country again to catch up with him. The chi kung research institute which had invited him to Tianjin then told me he had gone to Beijing on important business – to give a healing to a high-ranking official with Parkinson's disease. They also reported that he would have to spend at least two weeks in Beijing with the patient. And so, from Tianjin I went back to Beijing. Accompanied by Mr. Li Dongchu, editor of the Beijing magazine *Stamp Collecting* (he is a chi kung enthusiast too), I went to the hotel where the master was staying, explained my interest, and offered him a high fee to demonstrate his art. To eliminate any suspicion of trickery, I supplied my own candle and lit the flame myself. At no time did he touch the candle. He stood silently for about 20 seconds, gathering his chi. Then he pointed his finger at the candle flame for about three seconds, and the flame went out.

At that time, I asked him whether he could damage a person's eyes by pointing that amazing finger at them, and the answer was affirmative. However, he said that he had never tried it and didn't wish to, even on an animal. He told me: "I have practiced chi kung for 30 years and have full confidence in my power, so why would I need to do cruel and inhumane tests? When I point my fingers at acupuncture points to cure patients' diseases, the patients always feel something. Isn't that proof enough?" Satisfied with this answer, I went on to the following question: "Doesn't it hurt patients when you point your finger at their acupuncture points?" He replied: "It doesn't hurt a bit, because I can mentally control my power and adjust its constructive and destructive aspects to just the right mixture." Because I went through un-official channels and paid a high price to see this demonstration, I won't reveal this master's actual full name here.

## Master You in America

Early in 1981, Professor Martin Lee of Stanford University's physics department invited the empty force master from Shang-hai, You Pengxi (1902–1983), to visit the United States. Master You was a dermatology specialist who graduated from the medi-cal school of Shanghai's Tongji University and had also studied in Germany. Quiet by nature, he liked martial arts and had studied under many masters. When he heard how powerful Wang Xiangzhai's empty force was, he humbly requested to become his student and studied under Wang for many years.

As a result of this initial visit, You Pengxi started teaching classes in San Francisco's Fort Mason Center. He made a tremen-dous impression on the San Francisco martial arts community with his ability to knock down opponents without physical contact – a skill which led to a stormy debate in the pages of U.S. martial arts magazines. Nobody would believe in the art of knocking people down without physical contact, except those who had seen it with their own eyes.

You Pengxi died of diabetes at the age of 81. Because of the large number of people interested in the empty force, his wife carried on his teaching after his death. In an interview with a science reporter, she was asked whether the empty force was real and where its strange power came from. She gave a very good reply to this: "The only way to ascertain whether the empty force is real and how the power is produced is to learn it. You'll get to the bottom of it if you persist in practicing for three years."

I met her twice and personally observed how powerful her empty force was. However, she modestly claimed that it was only half as strong as her husband's had been. One of the late master's students once told me that on one occasion, in an empty force demonstration at Fort Mason, a 260-pound American came rushing at Master You, but as soon as the empty force master raised his hand and pointed at his assailant, the large and heavy-set man was stopped in his tracks.

## THE AMAZING POWERS OF WANG XIANGZHAI

In the 1920s, a master named Wang Xiangzhai appeared on the scene, and his fame spread all over China. He was the most famous master of the century since Yang Luchan, and he was also the master of my own teacher, Yu Yongnian.

*Figure 6 Master Yu Yongnian of Beijing demonstrates a yi quan posture*

Born in Hebei Province, Wang was a frail and sickly child who suffered from many diseases. Before he turned nine, his father sent him to practice martial arts fist-fighting under Guo Yunshen, who was at that time very famous for his *xin-yi* (mind and intention) style of fist art. The purpose of the training was to strengthen his physical condition. (In former times, martial arts was mainly used to improve health, while nowadays people practice martial arts for its own sake or for self-defense.) Master Yunshen was pleased with his student's sincerity and intelligence and, since he was getting old, he passed on all his secret martial arts techniques to Wang. After six years of study, without realizing it, Wang had mastered Yunshen's first-rate martial arts technique. However, he had no chance to put his skills to the test until one day (so the story goes), two years after completing his studies with Master Yunshen.

He was out on business with his father when he came across two monks outside a temple, having a practice match at martial arts to test each other's skill. Both of them were very powerful and they looked evenly matched. As Wang was enjoying the spectacle, the monks asked him if he had any martial arts knowledge himself. They asked him to join in and test his skill too. As soon as he went into action, his opponent was knocked to the ground. They tried again and the result was another knock down. Only then did he realize that he had mastered jing.

Jing is a very difficult concept to explain. It is the power of all the body's energy concentrated in a single point and released over a very short span of time. It also includes elements of elasticity and impact. Elasticity gives the ability to make a person bounce back a yard or two. Impact means that if the force comes into contact with the target's body or limbs, or with the stick or sword held by the target, he will be thrown to the ground as if feeling an electric shock.

The term "jing" should more correctly be called "jing of force" (i.e. martial arts force) which has two aspects: one exerted through physical contact and one without physical contact (as in the contest between the Japanese martial arts expert and Wang Xiangzhai described below). Because people consider knocking down an opponent without physical contact to be an extraordinary thing, they gave it the name of "empty force." Empty implies the absence of bodily or physical contact over a distance, as in "pushing the air to attack a person" (see p. 40).

*Figure 7    Master Wang Xiangzhai (Beijing 1960)*

After he became famous, Master Wang was hired as an instructor for China's Army Martial Arts Training Center. Once, he was sent to Shanghai, known as the "land of unknown supermen," to be the referee for a martial arts tournament there. Several masters asked for a match with him, and he knocked them all out easily.

The two best-known stories about Wang involve a Japanese and an Italian, each of whom came to China to challenge him to a match.

The first challenge took place in 1939, when Colonel Kenichi Sawai of the Japanese Army, a five-dan judo master and four-dan kendo master, came to Beijing to challenge Wang to a match, hoping to make a name for himself. Since Sawai was highly skilled in judo, he wanted to have a judo match with Master Wang. But as soon as Sawai started to fight, Wang knocked him back several feet. Wang's student Li Ying-Ang described it as "tossing him like a rubber ball." And so, the well-known Japanese colonel lost.

But Sawai still had his four-dan rank at kendo to fall back on. He imagined that Wang was only good at hand-to-hand fighting and not at sword-fighting, and that he would surely beat Wang in a fight with weapons. So he challenged Wang, producing a knife he had used for so many years that it was almost part of him. Against this, Wang just picked up a nearby stick. The result was that the fearsome Japanese master was sent flying "like a kite with a broken string." Still holding his knife, he was tossed up in the air and fell to earth several yards away. Sawai conceded the match.

Stunned that Wang had used only one move – a simple shaking of the stick – to throw him back so far, he asked Wang how he had done it. Wang replied: "An instrument or stick is an extension of the hand. If I can knock you down with my hand, then naturally I can do the same thing with a stick held in that hand."

In my opinion, the colonel's question missed the point. The most important element is "making the stick shake." This vibration is the jing mentioned earlier.

In any case, the colonel was convinced that Wang was a great master and asked to be his student. He wanted Wang to come to Japan to teach his art. Since this was during World War II and China was at war with Japan, Wang refused, agreeing only to teach the colonel in Beijing.

According to Li Ying-Ang, Wang asked another of his students, Yao Zongxun, to teach Sawai, and told him: "You shouldn't teach him the real art, but you mustn't say anything wrong and make us look ridiculous." In 1980, Li Ying-Ang went back to Beijing and asked Yao Zongxun about this occasion; but Yao didn't give a clear answer. As for Sawai, his book *Taikyokuken*, published in Japan in 1976, mentions the fearsome power of Wang's empty force.

One of the faults of many martial arts students is that they think that whatever they are studying is the best and can beat anything else. If they meet masters better than themselves, they feel unhappy and want to challenge them to a match. I don't know whether the Italians have ever heard of the Chinese saying, "For every mountain there is a higher mountain, and for every master there's a stronger master." If so, at least James, an Italian middleweight boxing champion, had not.

The second widely-known story concerning Wang's legendary powers tells how James came to China because he'd heard of the world-famous martial arts master. Having travelled all over China asking people to arrange a meeting, he finally got his wish. Their match was arranged. But as soon as the Italian started going into action, Wang tapped his arm and he fell to the ground instantly. He thought it was some kind of "magic," and didn't dare ask for a rematch. All he could do was admit defeat.

Because there are so many similar tales about Wang Xiangzhai, incorrect versions are sometimes told. According to some people, the one who fought with the Italian wasn't Wang himself, but Li Yongzong, a student of his. Wang is said to have had a more important engagement which he couldn't break, so he let Li go in his place. I believe this shows his superiority even more clearly; for, if his student could easily defeat the challenger, it implies that he himself must be all the more powerful – an idea he would wish to foster in order to discourage foreigners from coming to China and bothering him with challenges. In any case, people with the most highly developed art never like to make a display of it. The best Chinese martial arts masters are usually very friendly. They always keep in mind the thought that "for every mountain there is a higher mountain . . . ."

The empty force is obviously a super-powerful technique, but there may be an even more powerful technique. We will look into this issue in the section in Chapter 5, "The Highest Form of Martial Arts" (see p. 54).

Wang had hundreds of students over the course of his career, and about one out of 20 mastered the empty force. There are many reasons for this rather low success rate, not least because the technique is hard to understand, and the main method is difficult to master. Standing-on-stake alone is a highly demanding discipline for concentrating mind and spirit. It formed the basis of Yang Luchan's tai chi before he went on to develop tai chi postures; but he kept the secret of standing-on-stake to himself and his followers. But at all times the aim is to achieve a calm and happy state, a state of respect for and harmony with nature. A line from *The Yellow Emperor's Classic of Internal Medicine* reminds us of the same idea: "Maintain the self and the spirit."

Even among Chinese, very few people can master this, to say nothing of people from other cultures. One can only gain this type of wisdom through personal experience. The Italian boxer, of course, just like the Japanese, asked to become Wang's student. However, he gave up because he couldn't understand the philosophical basis of Chinese martial arts and couldn't fathom the mystery of standing-on-stake. After all, how could somebody who has spent over a decade jumping, moving and shaking the body around in a boxing ring have the patience to stand still for an hour several times a day?

## THE SECRETS OF YUE HUANZHI

Yue Huanzhi was another master, 20 years younger than Wang Xiangzhai, who had the same type of empty force skill. Initially, he studied under the famous tai chi master Tong Yingjie, who specialized in Yang Luchan's style of tai chi. Once, his teacher remarked: "Yang-style tai chi is famous and there are many teachers of it. Why did you choose me to be your teacher?" He replied, "I have great respect for people with real ability, not fakes with empty claims."

After that, Master Tong started to teach him in earnest, passing on all his secrets. Later, Master Tong went travelling and never returned. A few years after that, Yue studied the ways of Tibetan esoteric practices and learned some of their secret techniques. By combining tai chi and Tibetan esoteric practices, he mastered the empty force.

Yue Huanzhi lived in Shanghai, where he taught the empty force and did energy healing for people. He had a number of students, including one named Wang Yeh-Ling who now lives in Hong Kong. A letter of his about his teacher's career, published in the letters column of the Hong Kong journal *Da Cheng*, September 1985 (#142), revealed that Master Yue often had practice matches with his students and used these occasions to explain how to concentrate the mind to locate force and absorb or neutralize it (this is further explained in the discussion about "stopping a sparrow on the palm" on pp. 40–4). The more force an opponent uses to attack, the easier it is to knock him down or even make him fall down before he makes contact. Victims of this technique would be bounced off the walls like rubber balls or even hurled up to the ceiling, ending up on the floor. "I saw all this many times, and even tried it myself," he solemnly declared in his letter. As a public statement by one of Yue Huanzhi's satisfied students, this should be taken seriously.

Wang Yeh-Ling's description of his teacher's attacking

technique clearly relates to the empty force. However, Yue himself denied that he possessed empty force power, saying "I hate the words 'empty force.' In my village they have a bad meaning and are used for fakes and tricksters." Why would he deny he had the empty force? As explained elsewhere, the higher a master's level of skill, the less he admits it. This is a form of modesty. And besides, he could no more explain his power, as science demands, than the average person could explain where TV pictures come from. A fine example of this reticence comes from an empty force master living in Berkeley, California. He told his students not to mention the empty force, or "pushing the air to strike people," to Westerners. He believed that Americans are too scientifically minded to believe such things, and so he denied his skill.

Another reason for not wanting to reveal his empty force may have been that it is not equally effective on every opponent or "target." Not everyone will be bounced off the wall like a ball or thrown up to the ceiling. Those sensitive to chi will have that sort of reaction, but people without this sensitivity will move only a little, or not at all (but will actually be hurt more than the ones who are thrown around). If the master can't make the target move, then observers will say the master is a liar and the empty force is a fake.

Another awkward problem is that some people's power may not be at its peak, and may be unable to move the target or, at best, may be able only to hurt the target. In that case, the master had better deny that he has the empty force. Perhaps the best way to test for possession of the empty force would be to use measuring devices. (According to Mrs. You, in 1982 Stanford University professor Martin Lee and his team had plans to create such a device; but, unable to get enough funding for the project, they abandoned it.)

Master Yue, like the Berkeley master, publicly denied that he had the empty force, but it is an open secret among his supporters that during World War II he used the empty force to attack and seriously injure two Japanese soldiers.

Here is what is alleged to have happened: one day, four Japanese soldiers on the Nanjing Road in Shanghai were harassing a lady. When she cried out for help, a passer-by knocked down and seriously injured two of the soldiers – without physical contact. The other two soldiers hadn't heard any shot or seen anybody do anything violent, so, in a state of panic and confusion, all they could do was to close the road and declare it off-limits. They searched for quite some time, but failed to locate the culprit. When this story spread, everyone knew that it was Master Yue's handiwork, but they kept this to themselves.

Much later, Wang Yeh-Ling asked Master Yue whether he had in fact performed this deed. Neither confirming nor denying it, Master Yue gave an interesting answer: "No matter who did it, killing or injuring Japanese soldiers harassing ladies on the street would be a patriotic act."

# Chapter Four

# The Great Debate

It is part of human nature to debate. People are happy to debate almost any subject, from women's hairstyles to the extinction of the dinosaurs. In martial arts, we must be more cautious because of the fear of escalating from an argument to cursing and fighting. But if someone "calls a deer a horse" (as the Chinese refer to an outrageous claim), it can cause a debate all over the country.

In its thousands of years of history, the empty force has seen its share of controversy. It has even been debated outside of China – for example, in the United States where it is often greeted with skepticism because it runs counter to materialism and is not susceptible to the proofs of Western science. The only "proof" of the empty force's existence comes from acquiring it. But this, in turn, is problematical because it can only be attained by time, patience, and willpower – commodities that are all too often in short supply among Westerners. Few Americans, for instance, are willing to spare three to five hours a day to practice. More than this, it is also essential to cultivate a more spiritual outlook in which the mind is freed from materialism, personal and family problems are resolved, and the spirit is at peace. A shortcoming in any one of these areas will bring about failure. By contrast, in the rural lifestyle of ancient China, people had no conflicting desires and could devote themselves entirely to study. Naturally, the chances of succeeding were much higher. Even so, out of Wang Xiangzhai's hundreds of pupils, only about 30 or 40 learned the skill – and only six became powerful masters.

## THE FROG IN THE WELL

The April 1993 issue of the California magazine *Karate/Kung Fu Illustrated* contained an article by Jon Funk called "The Chilology Scam." He wrote that "to make a person jump or fall down without touching" is "nonsense." This gentleman distorts science into a kind of blind faith and superstitious rejection of the unknown. He says that "Chi kung practice simply cannot overcome the laws of physics," and, in the world of his science, "the law of physics" always requires physical contact. But he would do well to consider the analogy of radio waves – to say nothing of gravity and magnetism – which work within the "laws of physics" and yet need no "physical contact" to be effective.

Funk's article takes a simplistic approach to chi kung, considering it as just "basic breathing exercises." This ignores much of the respectable medical research about the effects of chi and chi kung. True, science has not yet been able to prove conclusively the existence of the empty force, but the serious scientific study of it is only in its infancy. Besides, it is only one of many phenomena which are considered nonexistent or even fraudulent because they cannot be proved according to the tenets of modern science.

After Jon Funk expressed his view, it was criticized by a master

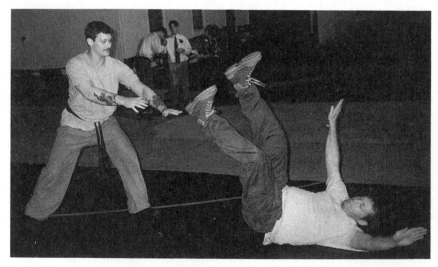

*Figure 8   Empty force masters can knock a person down without physical contact. Master Richard Mooney is one of them*

with long experience in the martial arts world: Richard Mooney of Florida. "I feel Funk did not do enough substantial research for his article," wrote Mooney. "I have been doing chi kung for years, and am able to push my students with chi alone." (See pp. 113–16 for more information on Mooney.)

The insulting language in Funk's article is provocative, and supporters of the empty force urged me to write the following refutation, entitled "Frog in the Well: Answer to a Man Trapped by Martial Arts," which I submitted to the same magazine. (It was not published, only because it came too long after Mr. Funk's article.) However, since it is relevant to the empty force debate, I would like to quote from it here:

> I don't usually like articles with baseless, sweeping statements (except as humor), but I made an exception in the case of Mr. Jon Funk's article which claims that to make someone move, jump, or fall down without touching them is nonsense. There is nothing unusual about invoking science to deny some extraordinary thing, but to use so many insulting terms such as "scam" or "fraud" to criticize chi kung and its masters shows that the gentleman lacks the spirit of chivalry and good manners proper to martial arts. It also shows the author's lack of experience and knowledge. During the classes of You Pengxi (1902–1983), an empty force master from Shanghai who came to the U.S. in 1981 to teach his amazing arts in San Francisco's Fort Mason Center, the students witnessed his use of the empty force to knock people down. It is true that this technique is only effective against one who is sensitive to chi, but about one out of every three people will be knocked down, pushed back, or made to sway. (For some reason I don't understand, the rate is higher for the master's own students, perhaps because of some harmony of the chi developed between the teacher and the student.) In any case, the effect certainly is achieved "without touching." If the gentleman would only go to China, he would find countless examples of such chi gong effects. He has no such experience, yet he makes sweeping statements. I call him a frog in the well.
>
> Those who live in the city may not understand what is meant by a "frog in the well." Allow me to explain. In ancient China, people did not have running water. The only source of water was to dig wells. But some wells were abandoned because they turned out to have no water. Sooner or later, a frog would make his home in such a well. The only thing the frog could see from there was a small part of the sky, not the world at large. Thus, people use the term "frog in the well" to refer to one with limited knowledge.
>
> More importantly, Mr. Funk, who loves martial arts, does not

appear to realize that anyone who wishes to practice martial arts must first build a foundation by practicing chi kung. Only in this way will the student be able to realize the most powerful martial arts. Long practice of chi kung will give rise to some inexplicable phenomena. Does a person who shows no familiarity with this common knowledge have the right to worship martial arts but say negative things about chi kung?

I picture him as someone who is so wrapped up in martial arts that he is trapped. All he knows is that the opponents must "touch" during a struggle. I must inform him that there are two kinds of force in martial arts: *shi jing* (solid force), which requires touching to have its effect, and *kong jing* (empty force), which has an effect even without touching. The former is effective on both those sensitive to chi and those who are not, while the latter is only effective on those sensitive to chi.

Another point, which I would like to emphasize strongly, is that both these forces are secrets of Chinese martial arts. The "empty force" was made public by Master You in San Francisco in 1981, while the "solid force" has not yet been revealed. The supreme Chinese arts are not usually taught to non-Chinese (whether or not

*Figure 9   Mrs You of San Francisco and Doc Fai Wong practicing empty force*

they should be goes beyond the scope of the current discussion). After my teacher's master, Wang Xiangzhai, knocked down a Japanese judo and kendo expert with a wave of the hand, the Japanese, Colonel Sawai, wanted to become Wang's student. Although Wang accepted, he had one of his students teach him – but he told the student not to teach the supreme arts.

Hasn't this martial arts fan, who likes to make sweeping statements, heard of this incident? He would do well to ask himself whether his own masters taught him their best arts. Perhaps his knowledge of martial arts doesn't include this maneuver.

Even if he has never heard of Wang Xiangzhai, could he really never have heard of the great tai chi master Yang Luchan? The reason he was attributed with the ability to "draw blood with every step" was that he first practiced *zhan zhuang* or standing-on-stake (a crucial part of chi kung) before graduating to tai chi. How many European and American teachers know this secret? The author is so bold as to make sweeping statements because he thinks he understands the whole story, but actually he doesn't know his own limitations. A Chinese motto says, "The most precious thing is to know oneself." Another old saying goes, "He who does not investigate and study has no place in the discussion." To deny something without bothering to test it goes against scientific principles. These words are all I wish to address to the frog in the well.

## THE CHINESE DEBATE

So far, the debate on the empty force in the United States has not spread much beyond the pages of the martial arts magazines, as in the above polemic. But we can now look back at the debate on the empty force within China itself.

Tai chi chuan in China is a broad subject. Not only do people enjoy it as a health practice, but chi kung and martial arts researchers are also fascinated by its mysteries. We have already mentioned that practicing tai chi is one of the ways of developing the empty force (see Chapter 7 for details); and this is one of the reasons for which it has attracted so much interest. There have been many works on tai chi in China's history, one of which is an anonymous work called *Taiji Quan Zong Shu (A Comprehensive Guide to Taiji Quan)*. This recounts a legend which is widely told in tai chi circles: that the famous tai chi master, Yang Luchan, could "paralyse a sparrow on his palm" and make it unable to fly away. According to this source, those who have practiced tai chi chuan for a long time develop such sensitive skin that they can absorb and dissipate the force and direction of the bird's thrust simply from the feel of its claws. It is as if the bird has no place against which to exert its leverage, and so it can't take off.

The same book also maintains that tai chi chuan as a fighting technique was forged in the same furnace as chi kung and martial arts. It involves directing chi with the mind. This can be combined with other energies and become a part of jing, or force. The highest masters need only concentrate their minds on a single point for chi to be spontaneously produced. This leads to stories of "pushing the air to strike people" which, in the tai chi world, is analogous to the empty force of chi kung.

The above leap from "stopping a sparrow in the palm" to "pushing the air to strike people" – another expression for the empty force – seems like science fiction, and naturally it is highly controversial. Thus, when a certain Zhang Jianzhong submitted an opinion to the "Public Forum" column of *Tiyu Bao* (*Sports News*), under the title of "From Stopping a Sparrow in the Palm to Pushing the Air to Strike People" (16 November 1985), he argued that when a bird takes off, its force is in the wings; and so, even if it can't get a grip on the palm, it will still be able to fly. Yang Luchan's ability to hold down a sparrow on his palm, he claimed, might be attributable to an electric charge from the body which attracts an opposite charge surrounding the bird. He explained that Chinese and ex-Soviet scientists have discovered in many experiments that a person's thought can exert a force on objects. He pointed out that there are subtle electric flows in the body, but the skin, with a resistance of 100 kilo-ohms, provides a layer of separation which seals them off from the external world. However, the electrical reactions of the skin are controlled by cerebral cortex cells so that some kind of thought, or a particular psychological state, can cause excitation of these cells and in this way lower the resistance of the skin, causing some organ or limb to release an electrical charge strong enough to envelop an object. If the object is giving off the same charge, it will be repelled; but if the charge is opposite, it will be attracted. This is how the body can exert a force beyond the ordinary physical abilities. Zhang Jianzhong makes a particular point of mentioning that our ancestors discovered this latent power of the body and called it *nei chi* (internal chi).

Although Mr. Zhang wrote quite a bit about "stopping a sparrow in the palm," his main argument concerned "pushing the air to strike people," – that is, the empty force. He held that "pushing the air to strike people" is a dangerous expression, that the empty force is a "mystic art," and that such claims should not be made lightly for fear of being labeled as superstitious nonsense. In ancient times, people had no scientific knowledge and so they thought that knocking down or injuring people without physical contact was not a natural power, but some kind of spirit which, emanating from the body, moved the air to attack the target. Nowadays it ought to be possible to set such a phenomenon on a firmer scientific footing.

Zhang also expressed the deep conviction that in both tai chi and chi kung, thought power plays a major role and can give rise to "power beyond the ordinary physical realm." The palm power of tai chi chuan and the "pushing the air to strike people" of the empty force both come from thought power, but we must investigate and verify this scientifically rather than blindly promoting it.

When Mr. Zhang's opinion was voiced, it provoked letters in response from several readers. Some said they had never seen "pushing the air to strike people," and wouldn't believe it even if they saw it. Exerting force on a person without physical contact, they said, is nothing but a magic trick. Others said there are all kinds of strange things in this great world, so they would believe it if they saw it with their own eyes. Still others said they had studied martial arts for 20 years and had never heard of this.

Some time later, Deputy Director Lu Wuwen, of the Chinese Medicine Department of Guangzhou City Railway Hospital, published an article called "More on Pushing the Air to Strike People." His main thrust was that, although he had practiced tai chi chuan for 50 years, he had never mastered thought, chi, and jing, so he didn't know how "pushing the air to strike people" could work and believed it was nonsense. But having studied *wuji* (boundless) style chi kung (see glossary) under the Guangzhou empty force master Cai Songfang, he had gradually come to learn these mysteries. A few years later, he found himself able to "push the air to strike people." "When I send chi at an opponent by waving my hand at him," he wrote, "he flies several meters back. I can even send chi through walls or through large trees and the opponent still falls back." He is firmly convinced that this is a latent power of the body developed by *wuji* style chi kung and that "pushing the air to strike people" is real. He also remarked that although the power is real it can be strong or weak.

Dr. Lu went on to describe four types of sensitivity to chi – high, medium, low, and no sensitivity – which could be defined by the different reactions to chi emitted by a chi kung master. If the master sends chi from his hands at a person with high sensitivity, the target will be pushed back violently. Such a person can even be made to jump around when simply standing near a chi kung master who is directing chi at someone else. A person of medium sensitivity will be pushed back by direct chi from the master, but not affected indirectly. One of low sensitivity will experience strong heart thumping, chest discomfort, or dizziness; and one of no sensitivity will not feel anything, although there may be internal injury.

Since publication of his article, I have been introduced to Dr. Lu, and we have often exchanged letters. He has told me that we must not use intuition and subjective judgement to research the truth or falsehood of the empty force. What appears to the eye is not always the truth. One must practice it oneself to prove its reality. For this reason, he believes that it is useless to argue with one who has never practiced it. He has introduced many of his friends to this technique, hoping to build up a larger group to practice together and have more fun. But most of them find it difficult to believe.

Also after Dr. Lu's letter came out, another reader, Zhu Sijia, contributed to the debate. He was a friend of the great empty force master Yue Huanzhi who, like Yang Luchan three hundred years before, had obtained his power through tai chi. Together with Wang Xiangzhai, these masters are unsurpassed, their power – as the Chinese say – out of this world.

Zhu Sijia's article agreed that manifestations of the empty force, whether "stopping a sparrow in the palm" or "pushing the air to strike people," should be scientifically studied. But of their reality he had no doubt. In the 1950s, he had seen Master Yue "make people stand motionless in front of him, clearly a stronger power than stopping a sparrow on the palm. Using the empty force, he could knock down several strong opponents without physical contact."

## MASTER WANG'S PALM

The final testimony to "stopping a sparrow in the palm" and "pushing the air to strike people" comes from Zong Fangshan, a consultant for the "Chi Gong Meditation and Physical Training Society" of Toronto, Canada. In an article in the journal *Chi Gong*, published in Hangzhou, he said that "stopping a sparrow in the palm" was an indisputable fact and he had seen it with his own eyes, performed by the famous Wang Xiangzhai. He said the master lived in Ye County, Shandong Province, and he came home once a year. In 1934, the government of Ye County requested the returning Master Wang to perform his rarely-demonstrated technique of "stopping a sparrow in the palm." Zong Fangshan had a chance to watch the demonstration because he was then working in the top level of the county government. The audience was full of high-ranking officials, and it wasn't open to the general public. He described the master, then in his 80s, as having a glowing face, sparkling eyes, and a crisp voice. As he strode briskly into the room, it could be seen at a glance that here was a master of the Way. As he recalled it, Master Wang put a lively sparrow on his smooth palm. The bird started fluttering, but the master made many deft palm motions downward, and the sparrow was unable to take off. Then it started squawking and flapping more and more strongly, but Master Wang's palm followed along in constant motion. In the end, the hopping bird was unable to escape from Master Wang's palm. Because Zong was in the audience for this rare performance, he took the opportunity to ask Master Wang why the sparrow couldn't fly away. The master explained: "Whenever a bird takes off, it has to push its claws against the ground. It can't fly just by flapping its wings, without pushing off against the ground." From this, Mr. Zong judged that Master Wang had practiced tai chi for many years and achieved great mastery, such that every cell in his body had the utmost sensitivity. When the sparrow pushed its claws down, Master Wang instantly reacted by sinking his palm inward. The bird's claws had nothing to push against, leaving it fluttering ineffectively and unable to fly away. As the bird moved to a new position and pushed again, Master Wang again made his palm sink inward. In this way, adjusting his palm to the sparrow's thrusts, he completely dissipated their force. According to Mr. Zong, these subtle palm motions are the secret of reacting to one's opponent in tai chi fists, and such sensitivity can only come with the highest level of mastery. Incidentally, with the becoming reluctance of a true master, Wang had no desire to perform on this occasion. He agreed to do so only after repeated requests from the president and all the instructors of the Ye County Martial Arts Institute, along with heads of other organizations.

As to whether Master Wang used his power (or agility) to prevent sparrows from flying, or whether it was an effect of the electric charge from his palms, that is another matter. I believe it is the latter. This is not to say that the master was tricking the public. This incident took place in the 1930s, and Master Wang had no knowledge of bioelectricity in the human body. That is why he believed it was the power of his palm preventing the sparrows from flying off. However, I have done an experiment on this myself. I went to the park and threw out some bread crumbs to lure a pigeon, caught it and held it in my hand. Then, I hurled it toward the sky. The instant I flung it, the bird opened its wings and flew away. This proves that traction against the palm is not necessary for flying. True, at the riverside I often see water fowl pushing against the water as they take off, because they have clumsy bodies. As they open their wings, they paddle furiously in the water at least 20 to 30 times before they can take off. This indicates that the sparrow, with its light body, doesn't need to push against any solid object to fly, unlike clumsy heftier birds.

We hope this book will not be the end of the debate, but that it will continue in any Western sports magazine, martial arts magazine, chi kung magazine, or tai chi magazine. Although we may be in different parts of the world, separated by oceans, we can communicate with our spirits and our pens about these ancient and modern stories of pushing the air to strike people. It is certain to be interesting.

Chapter Five

# Martial Arts, Tai Chi and Chi Kung

## MARTIAL ARTS

Some people would say that martial arts have lost their status and usefulness since the invention of the handgun. This simplistic attitude shows no appreciation of artistic value. As we all know, in the century since the introduction of the handgun, martial arts have not only survived, they are being taken more and more seriously. It used to be only large cities that had martial arts schools, but now we find them even in small towns. This shows that martial arts have preserved their exalted position over the millennia.

They are not only for self-defense, but also for the promotion of health; not only for macho tough-guys interested in fighting, but for anyone, including women. One day, while working on this book, I went to a performance of the "Official Beijing Martial Arts Team," a group of 16 martial artists on a tour of the United States. The large auditorium was filled to capacity. About one-third of the people in the audience, and seven of the performers, were women. Since women have more flexible bodies, they are able to develop superior abilities in some aspects of martial arts. Jumping high, twirling and sparring, the performers won constant applause from the audience. Then, five women appeared and gave a smooth and graceful demonstration of tai chi, moving in perfect unison. Tai chi's rhythmic movements contain strength within softness; its smooth flow is like a cloud or a stream of water. Its high artistry dazzled the audience and led to further cries of acclaim.

Martial arts, tai chi, and chi kung are three forms of the same essence, just like water, steam, and ice. Each has the same source, but each has different powers, so that they are at once independent and interconnected. This is the Chinese principle of yin and yang – many opposing things in life are interdependent. Martial arts concentrate on hard fighting, coming right out at the start with striking fists and kicking legs. This approach is characterized by swift, nimble motions with the aim of deciding the battle quickly. Tai chi is just the opposite. It has the power to beat the hard with the soft. Images of water putting out fire, or a woman winning over a man, are frequent metaphors for the "softness" of tai chi overcoming the "hardness" of martial arts. Martial arts enthusiasts often prefer to see the movements of tai chi as slow and unable to compete with their discipline, but they underestimate this "soft" power of tai chi.

In 1962, a contest between a martial arts master and a tai chi master, billed as a battle to the death, was held in Macao (about 40 kilometers from Hong Kong). This event received major media coverage in both Macao and Hong Kong, and the public was in suspense over the outcome. Each discipline had its ardent supporters but in the event, they fought to a tie. The judges awarded victory to both sides, and everyone was satisfied with the result. In the battle between the hard and the soft, both sides have some wins and some losses. That is why a wise person would wish to figure out a way to combine them, together with chi kung, and so create a practice of unimaginable power – the power, in fact, of the empty force.

What makes the empty force so devastating? Its technique is very simple. The training consists in combining thought with body energy. We would do well to consider the example of yi quan (intention fist). Yi quan, as we have seen, is a combination of martial arts and chi kung. It involves physical contact and uses the fists to strike a target. In this sense it is not an empty force practice, but because it trains the mind power and develops the chi, it can be part of a practice leading to the empty force. Yi quan uses the power of the mind to make use of muscles which are not ordinarily used. For example, it trains the flexor and extensor muscles. In this manner, the whole is greater than the sum of its parts. One person can develop the power of two people combined. And the power of two people combined can be greater than the two taken separately, and can even reach the power of

*Figure 10   Empty force master Mrs You practices the technique of knocking out an opponent with one blow*

three people. The strangest thing is that although yi quan normally requires physical contact to have an effect, those who attain the highest mastery can produce the empty force's effect, knocking down an opponent without physical contact. This is difficult for us to understand. There must be some transformation involved, such as an energy transformation, but it is still difficult for science to explain it. For this reason, some practitioners of yi quan deny the existence of the phenomenon, while most of them are only interested in attaining the power without being concerned where it comes from.

The empty force is more than just the combination of martial arts and chi kung or martial arts and tai chi, in the same way that a mother and father give birth to a child but the child has its independent life. Just as children can be seen as having the same characteristics as their parents, but are more intelligent, more flexible and stronger, so, analogously, the empty force is born from the martial arts practice of yi quan or tai chi in combination with chi kung meditation.

The Qing Dynasty tai chi master Yang Luchan attained the empty force by such a combination, adding standing-on-stake (the basic form of yi quan) to tai chi. This is why he was so powerful and was reputed to be able, we remember, to "draw blood with a single gesture." Yang was the chief of the "Special Skills Force," the palace guards for the Chinese emperor, and he made sure all his troops practiced standing-on-stake. Under his training, the force became a fearsome team of top masters. In those days, the mere mention of the words "Special Skills Force" would strike terror into people's hearts. Unfortunately, only a few of the people now teaching tai chi understand this principle of learning standing-on-stake before tai chi. However, this is not to say that everyone who adds standing-on-stake to tai chi will master the empty force. It depends on several factors – the length of time spent practicing, whether or not the mind guides the chi, what forms of tai chi are practiced, and so on.

Master Yue Huanzhi, introduced in Chapter 3, attained the empty force through tai chi practice, but only after he had studied a Tibetan esoteric Buddhist tradition. The point here is that while tai chi combined with standing-on-stake is the best path to the empty force, tai chi combined with chi kung meditation is equally valid. Yue didn't think he would learn the empty force from esoteric Buddhism, and he knew that tai chi alone wouldn't give rise to the empty force. For this reason, he didn't consider himself an empty force master. Besides, he was afraid he would be accused of practicing black magic instead of tai chi if people said he could "push the air to strike people." He forbade his students to mention the words "empty force," even though he actually was a very powerful empty force master.

There are many interesting stories about Yue Huanzhi. Here is one of them: Harton, a wealthy Jew who owned a whole street in Shanghai at one time, employed several very strong martial arts masters as bodyguards. One day, Harton invited Yue to a banquet. At the banquet table, he requested that Yue demonstrate his skills against one of his bodyguards. Yue politely refused, but the bodyguard felt superior and wanted to show off in front of his boss. He kept pestering Yue with his challenges, and Harton encouraged Yue by saying, "Don't worry about hurting or killing my man. I'll take responsibility for that." Yue continued to refuse, but the bodyguard unexpectedly attacked him. Yue immediately dodged his charge and poked him in the side, breaking a rib. The bodyguard fell to the ground. Harton was convinced and gave up. However, the next day Harton sent a limousine to take Yue to another banquet. Yue imagined it would lead to another challenge, so he told the chauffeur: "Your master is very rich! Let him buy a dog for a playmate. I'm not a toy for him to play with."

After Yue became famous, many people came to study with him. One of these was named Doung Bing. He had already mastered powerful Shaolin techniques and was well-known, so he often practiced with Yue. Other students enjoyed watching their sparring too, because it was a spectacular scene. One day, when Yue was sparring with Doung Bing, he asked Doung to come at him with all his strength. But as soon as this powerful attack was mounted, Yue was afraid he'd be unable to defend himself, so he used the empty force. Doung felt a wave of power and, frozen with terror, fell to the ground. This was when Yue realized that the jing, or force, he had sent out was too strong. He quickly helped Doung to his feet. Later, Doung told his fellow students that jing is a fearsome thing, like an irresistible attack by some sort of evil sorcery. He couldn't describe how he felt.

I have often asked my students and friends for their impressions of this indescribable sensation mentioned by Doung. They all say it is indeed hard to describe precisely. Once, in 1989, I visited a class of Master Cai Songfang's empty force students in Berkeley, California, during their practice session. I asked Dr. Sandy Rosenberg from the University of California what it felt like when Master Cai used the empty force on him. He agreed that it is hard to describe, saying "I feel something very strange and have to get away from it." Some students told me they experienced an unpleasant sensation and felt nauseous, dizzy, confused, or upset. There was some unbearable power which made them lose all ability to resist. Others described it as like entering a magnetic field.

Colonel Kenichi Sawai, whom we met in Chapter 3, has also tried to describe the sensation of being assailed by the empty force. In his book *Taikyokuken* he writes: "That instant, I completely lost control of my hands and fell down. I don't know what made me fall, but I experienced a sharp pain like an electric shock, and my heart felt like I had been struck by lightning. I was attacked by a strange, stunning power I'd never felt before, and it was terrifying."

As a martial art, the empty force is quite different from ordinary martial arts and cannot be compared with them. The hundreds of available books on martial arts mostly deal with particular forms and techniques, with their attack and counters. If two masters of

*Figure 11   Paul Dong (center) showing his Y.M.C.A. students how to practice standing-on-stake*

such techniques meet, they can struggle for over an hour. But the power of the empty force lies in its single form, which ends the fight after one or two moves. It only takes a few seconds. In ordinary martial arts, a person can learn enough to start competing in fights after one year of training, and those with greater patience can wait two or three years before getting into the arena. But for the empty force, the basic training is three years, but it takes five or six years to achieve a high level of power. To become a master, and attain extraordinary powers, takes ten years. This is the difference between ordinary martial arts and the empty force.

## TAI CHI

I would like to emphasize that whoever understands tai chi, or wants to achieve better results, must first practice standing-on-stake. This strengthens the legs, providing a firm foundation for action, and ultimately gives rise to internal jing (force), which can improve the effectiveness of the fighter's advancing and retreating, dodging or standing firm, counter-attacking, and so on. However, in my experience, more than half of the people in the practice are unaware of this and consider tai chi and standing-on-stake as two different things – as if the latter were a part of martial arts of chi kung, but not of tai chi.

*Figure 12 Tai chi master Gregory Fong in one of the standing-on-stake postures. He is working on building up his jing (power)*

Nevertheless, in a sense it is true that tai chi is a beneficial exercise which can be undertaken for its own sake. But, if you want to develop internal jing, you must practice standing-on-stake. Start by doing the standing exercise for five minutes at a time and gradually increase it to half an hour, only starting the tai chi practice after completing the standing exercise. Standing-on-stake should be practiced for at least 15 minutes. In practicing yi quan or other forms of empty force, 45 minutes of practice are the minimum. This is explained further in Chapter 7.

Long practice of standing-on-stake leads to jing, the main power of the empty force. Releasing jing is a sure way to knock down an opponent. This is also the reason that the empty force is such a fearsome technique. But we must be clear about the distinction between jing and li (strength). They are impossible to define precisely because of the difficulty in translating Chinese into English – quite apart from the fact that they can really only be grasped through direct personal experience. However, li comes from the body and is present at birth. Even without practicing any martial arts, tai chi or chi kung, a person has li. It may be thought of as energy, strength, power, force, etc. Jing, on the other hand, can only come from practice, notably that of tai chi or standing-on-stake. Moreover, jing usually comes from the muscles rather than the body. When we practice either the empty force or yi quan, we use the mind to strengthen the muscles of the arms and legs. Gradually, the muscles are not only strengthened, but they also develop jing.

Further differences between the two can be expressed in this way: li is diffuse while jing is focused; li is floating around but jing is packed down and ready to explode; li is coarse but jing is fine; li is rectilinear, strained, and slow while jing is rounded, free-flowing, and fast. More importantly, li is tangible but jing is intangible. For example, if I hit you, the fist has to land on you to have any effect (cause pain), and the action is visible to the eye. This is the tangible strength of li. A force that doesn't need to hit you and has its effect instantly is intangible, like jing. It could be likened to a powerful blast from a bomb exploding near you. Even though none of the fragments from the explosion hit you, the shock waves can injure you. The impact of an explosion comes from all sides (li is diffuse), but the jing in the empty force comes in one packet (jing is focused).

I once asked three empty force masters their feelings about jing. One of them said, "Like an arrow"; another said, "like a spring recoiling"; and the third said, "like a car's bumper, concentrating all the force of the car in a single point." It's hard for me to say which description is the most appropriate. This is something which can only be understood by experiencing it for oneself.

A chapter "On Jing" in Chen Gong's *Taiji Quan Pu* says: "When the hand is in place, the jing comes; before it is in place there is no jing, and after it passes its place there is no jing. At just the moment it is in place, it is as quick as lightning." In other words, the power has all its effect in the one moment it is released. This gives an approximate description of sending jing and being hit by it. If we consider the meaning of the phrases "when the hand is in place, the jing comes," and "quick as lightning," won't those who claim that a handgun is the ultimate weapon need to reconsider their views?

Chen Gong also discusses ling kong jing (the empty force). This jing, he says, is very mysterious, almost mystical, and something which has to be witnessed to be believed. When a high master releases jing with a cry, the target feels unsteady on his feet or steps back, unable to offer any resistance.

This explains the relationship of tai chi to martial arts and standing-on-stake. Now let us turn to a discussion of chi kung.

## CHI KUNG

Chi kung is the foundation of martial arts and tai chi, and has a broad range of applications. One wishing to practice martial arts should first practice chi kung. Failure to do so leads to strength without chi – a physical, but not spiritual, strength. Unfortunately, many practitioners of martial arts neither practice chi kung, nor even try to distinguish one from the other. I have seen even more preposterous martial arts teachers. As soon as the words "chi kung" are mentioned, they shout: "What do you mean, chi kung? Let me have a match with them, I'll knock them right down." Knowledgeable listeners are amused by this. Of course, if you don't take the basics seriously – that is to say, if you don't take the source of power seriously – you can make the mistake of separating chi kung from martial arts. This is much the same as the ignorant tai chi instructors who separate standing-on-stake from tai chi.

Like tai chi, chi kung is "soft," whereas martial arts are "hard." But both martial arts and tai chi place the main emphasis on action (with the exception of yi quan), while chi kung focuses on stasis. Its forms are classified as standing, sitting, or lying, but while performing these positions one must achieve three conditions – relaxation, quietness and emptiness. After maintaining these for a certain period of time (usually over 15 minutes), one will find that the cerebral cortex is calmed, the body enters a peaceful and comfortable state, the blood circulation is enhanced, the metabolism is enlivened, and the increased blood circulation brings abundant oxygen to the cells. This provides an improved distribution of energy to all parts of the body. With such energy, health is preserved, the spirit is invigorated, and sickness can be cured (especially in the case of chronic illnesses). This is why "chi kung therapy" is popular in Mainland China, with millions of people practicing it every day.

Because chi kung is static while tai chi is active, the former trains "chi" (energy) while the latter trains the muscles and physique. But, together, chi kung and tai chi can compensate for each other's deficiencies and achieve better results for health and healing. Now, if chi kung is combined with martial arts instead of tai chi, what are the results? In a word, yi quan. Other types of empty force have the same basis – the development of chi combined with the action of the mind ("guiding chi with mind") in order to produce their uncanny effects. Thus, chi kung is useful for health and healing as well as for martial arts and self-defense. It also costs nothing, although it does require a great deal of time and patience.

I have written a 70,000-word book with Dr. Esser called *Chi Gong: An Ancient Chinese Way to Health*, which was published in the United States recently. I still have enough material to write another 100,000-word book, because chi kung is a vast subject which has captured the attention of ancients and moderns, Chinese and non-Chinese alike. However, in this chapter, the main focus has been on the combination of martial arts, tai chi, and chi kung to produce self-defense effects. If the reader would like to learn more about chi kung, there are about a dozen books on the subject in print in the United States and Britain. So, we will not dwell on it further here.

## THE HIGHEST FORM OF MARTIAL ARTS

Of course, in my own view, the empty force is the highest existing form of martial arts in China. However, the limitations of one man's opinion should be recognized. There could always be some higher art I haven't heard of. In addition, I would like to point out that nothing is absolute in this world. If an empty force master went around attacking everybody, he might meet his match one day. A Chinese proverb goes, "There are people above people, and there are heavens beyond Heaven." The more adept a master's skill at martial arts, the more will he shun publicity and keep that skill hidden. The Chinese are a peace-loving people, and martial arts are considered as a health exercise and defensive technique, a means for self-development, not self-aggrandizement.

In ancient times, if you wanted to study a powerful art, you were required to take an oath to observe the rules of martial arts ethics. Candidates had to swear not to show off their power; to use the power for defensive and not aggressive purposes; and to use the power to help the weak against the strong and do good deeds. A teacher would not take lightly the responsibility of passing on knowledge of a technique. The most important consideration would be the character of the student. Only those of high moral character would be accepted.

Also, the strength of the power depends on how much time is spent practicing it. It is inevitable that one who practices six hours a day will develop stronger power than one who practices three hours a day. To give an example: in recent years, Chinese athletes have broken many world records and won many gold medals. It is possible to account for this in three ways: first, rigorous training; second, extended periods of training; and third, the athletes being forbidden to visit with friends, relatives, and especially spouses, because it might disturb their concentration. This is the only way to maintain the focus – something Western athletes rarely accomplish – and is one of the secrets of the success of the physically smaller Chinese against the physically more powerful Westerners. Diligent practice, confidence, and concentration are always decisive factors.

At the same time, the Chinese believe "all things in the world counterbalance each other." According to this viewpoint, the universe is something like a huge system of checks and balances. Everything has its opposite side, every action has its reaction. Water can overcome fire, rust can corrode steel, the yin (negative) and yang (positive) principles are always keeping each other under control. If there are too many rats and snakes on the planet, hawks will appear to prey on them and keep the population under control. Even the spiralling growth of human population is counterbalanced by natural disasters, self-destructive activities by humans themselves, and disease. According to this logic, there must be some medicine or technique to beat those terrible scourges, cancer and AIDS. We just haven't learned what it is yet.

For decades, I have been following stories of people with special abilities in China's chi kung and martial arts worlds, and I have spent a great deal of time and money in visiting these amazing people. My contacts in the martial arts world have told me, for example, that there is a hermit living on China's Mt. Emei who has the ability to evade visitors (even the hard-to-evade journalists). It is claimed that he uses his keen spiritual powers to sense when someone is coming and so gets away. If people with bad intentions want to come to hurt him, he runs away and leads them on a wild goose chase. Eventually, they get tired of the useless pursuit. It is also said that there is a mystic who has the power to draw a circle around himself to repel enemies. He sits in the center of it, and if anyone with evil intent tries to come in, the intruder will be dazed, nauseous, unsteady on the feet, and will finally collapse. Yet another report describes a man in Hunan province who can make you lose your fighting strength just by looking you over for a while.

I strongly believe in the existence of such martial arts skills, which make use of mind power to overcome an opponent, because the empty force which I learned also contains the same elements.

There is really no way of telling which of the martial arts is the highest – and who is the most powerful exponent. In 1994, China had a population of 1.2 billion people. Among these, there must be all kinds of people with mysterious powers. As such, it would be superficial to compare two or three examples to try to find which one is the most proficient. If we want to look more deeply at the art of fighting, there is a saying in *Sun-Tzu's Art of War*, an ancient Chinese text now found in the libraries of many military academies around the world (even if they haven't learned its lessons): "The best policy is to let others weaken themselves by fighting." Another ancient Chinese proverb says, "Nothing can oppose kindness." By being good to others, you will have no enemies. Thus, "kindness" is the world's greatest defensive art. If you combine these two concepts – "Let others weaken themselves by fighting" and "Nothing can oppose kindness" – you will master the deepest mystery.

If these sayings don't capture your imagination, perhaps a bit of wisdom known to every household in China will help: "For every gain there will be a loss." No matter what you attain, it will carry with it some cost – rather like the American saying,

"You win some, you lose some." For example, if a man marries a beautiful woman, she may be proud, hard to get along with, and so attractive to other men that a rival may come and break up the family. Or let us suppose that you hit the jackpot in the lottery. You will get rich, live in a mansion and drive a luxury car; but at the same time you will worry about thieves attacking you, lose your peace of mind, and have trouble sleeping at night.

By the same token, if you really want to be a world-class martial artist, you will have to sacrifice some of the time that could otherwise have been spent in the enjoyment of family life, and you will also inspire jealousy in rival martial artists. As the saying goes, "Be satisfied with what you have," and enjoy the mysteries of the empty force.

Chapter Six

# The Healing Power

In the 23 January 1995 issue of the American magazine *Business Week*, an article was published under the title: "They Fly Through the Air with the Greatest of ... *Ki*?" The article describes the use of *ki* (the Japanese translation of chi) for health purposes with a practice that sounds similar to that of the empty force. According to the article, Japanese chi kung master Kozo Nishino has a health practice in which he sends people flying through the air with his chi. His clients are said to include many top Japanese corporate executives. The article includes a photograph of Nishino waving his hand at a student, who is flying away from him. (By the way, it also mentions that many Japanese research institutes, including the laboratories of the Sony Corporation and the Ministry of International Trade and Industry, are now studying practical applications of chi.) Such use of a chi kung master's chi to strengthen the health of a patient is the theme of this chapter.

## ENERGY HEALING

For me, energy healing is one of the most interesting topics. I enjoy having the ability to help others. Although I have mastered the energy healing powers, I do not advertise in the papers to do it for money. This would bring me some cash but dissipate my power (which is like a car's battery, and can be weakened through excessive use). Instead of using it for money-making, this power can be properly used to do healings for the benefit of close friends and relatives.

I remember the first time I gave a healing to a family member suffering from pain. It was in 1987. It took a few seconds for the patient to feel the chi in the painful area. After about three minutes, the pain disappeared, and the patient felt very relaxed as well. For this, I was praised highly: "Relieving someone's pain is a good deed." I was very pleased to hear this, of course. Another time, I gave a healing to a friend with a skin problem. As I sent my chi to the affected part, the back of her hand, she felt the chi move up the arm to her shoulder, and then downwards, via her stomach, to the *dan tian* point (around the navel). She also felt a comforting stream of warmth going through her body, causing her to exclaim: "How did you get this fantastic power? It is a wonderful healing technique." I was delighted by her praise.

On another occasion, I was giving chi kung lessons to several members of the Foundation for Mind-Being Research in Los Altos, California. The secretary of the foundation, Mrs. Marion Gough, is sensitive to chi. While she was doing meditation, I sent external chi toward the "third eye" point on the forehead (above the nose). After finishing the meditation, she told me that she not only felt great, but also that she had seen a green "healing light" glowing in front of her forehead. I would rather receive such praise than a hundred dollars (some famous Chinese healers *do* charge a hundred dollars for a healing!)

Another experience of mine concerned a visiting professor from Germany who requested that I give her an energy healing. She was accompanied by an American woman who was preparing to participate in the Olympic javelin-throwing event. Imagine the physique of a javelin thrower compared to a slightly built Chinese man! It was like a meeting of a giant and a midget. I had them stand side by side in order to demonstrate my chi on them. Because they were both so large, I concentrated strongly when sending out my chi. At once they fell back on the bed placed behind them to avoid being injured. They pronounced the experience "amazing."

One of my most satisfying experiences has been my association with Dr. Myles Suehiro. He is a lung specialist living in Hawaii, and in recent years he has been coming to San Francisco every year for a medical congress. Whenever he comes, he calls me to his hotel to restore his chi. He understands that restoring chi is just like recharging a battery for a car. After I restore his chi for 20 minutes, he feels like his whole body is full of energy, his spirit is high, and he sleeps better at night. "These are things money can't buy." I am delighted to hear these words of praise from him. When I, in turn, expressed my admiration of doctors, he said, "Any human skill is worthy of admiration. The ability to do energy healing should be seen as a medical skill." These words have been a tremendous encouragement; and, since then, I have prized my ability and worked hard to develop it further.

## MEASURING CHI

It was Dr. Suehiro who introduced me to Professor William Tiller of Stanford University's Materials Science Department for the purpose of measuring my energy with an extremely sensitive instrument he had invented. I had always wanted to do scientific tests to prove my abilities, but Professor Tiller was busy writing a science textbook at the time and we were unable to arrange the experiment. Later, I found an experimental scientist at Lawrence Berkeley Laboratory, Dennis DiBartolomeo, who *was* able to do the test. He had one of Professor Tiller's instruments, called a gas discharge cell apparatus, which, allegedly sensitive to chi, is indispensable for testing human body energy and energy fields.

According to its inventor, the device "seemed to register influence by human energy fields/human consciousness." The principle is similar to that of Kirlian photography, but the high voltage potential is maintained at a stable level, and the gas and discharge are in a sealed chamber to insulate them from changes in the atmosphere. Consisting of a "thin film of gas between the glass plates of a sealed chamber which was subjected to a high AC voltage potential," the apparatus has shown (according to Tiller) that "anomalous discharges occurred when human attention was focused on [it]." In other words, he showed that the mind seems to have some ability to influence electrical effects in the physical world – an influence which penetrated ordinary shielding, and could not be imitated by any mechanical device he tried. Moreover, he was able to repeat this experiment on several different people with similar results. The experiment on me, incidentally, showed that my energy reached 3675 volts . . .

What does this prove? Dennis DiBartolomeo speculated that

"the cause could be classified as a bioenergetic field (called chi in Chinese medicine) effect or a 'psychic' phenomenon (i.e. an effect of consciousness on matter at a quantum level which influences the discharge)." In the same letter to me he speculates further about the measurable effects of chi at the gas/glass interface, whose extreme sensitivity may perhaps register quantum effects or act like a biological cell membrane.

Here is what he wrote about the test in which I sent chi to his apparatus:

> I . . . have seen increases in discharge during and right after a 15 min. period during which time the subject attempts to focus attention on or direct energy to the discharge cell. This effect was also noticed following a 15 min. "directed energy" period during your visit on 17 August '93. This period, which started at ~15:00 . . . occurred when the discharge rate had been decreasing for over 90 min. The discharge rate right after the "directed energy" period shows a noticeable increase. This increase drops off over the next couple of hours.

Thus chi, it seems, is detectable by modern scientific methods, and I hope this type of research will be continued and expanded in the future so that we will learn to measure chi.

On 26 March 1993, I drove to Los Altos, California to attend Professor Tiller's lecture on "Subtle Energies." His lecture covered three main points: (1) Experiments exploring the human body as a transmitter/receiver for electromagnetic subtle energies; (2) Techniques for the reliable detection of subtle energies; and (3) The role and value of energy medicine, present and future. There was not an empty seat in the lecture hall that evening. Scientific work such as his is beginning to supply a theoretical explanation for energy healing within the tenets of modern science.

I have continued to seek out chances to do experiments to obtain further proof of my healing energy. On 18 May 1989, Dr. Chu, an acupuncturist who was taking my chi kung class in the San Francisco YMCA, introduced me to San Francisco's Computerized Thermographic Imaging – a system of measuring and visually displaying the amount of heat emitted by a body. An image was produced of my hand transmitting chi on to someone's knee in the course of a healing session. The hand showed an increase in temperature of 0.5°C, while the leg's temperature rose by as much as 1.1°C – both statistically significant results.

Machines are not the only way to detect a person's energy.

Some people can see it with their eyes. It is estimated that one or two percent of people can see chi. I have a friend and two students who tell me they can see chi in my palms or coming from my fingers whenever I send it. Of course, friends and students may have a psychological predisposition to see this. However, one complete stranger – a bone specialist and chi kung master called Dr. Wang Yingqiu – once approached me after a chi demonstration and remarked: "Master Dong, I can see your chi is very strong and is the color white." I asked what it looked like, and he said, "a straight line moving forward."

## DEVELOPING CHI

As the saying goes, "there's no such thing as a free lunch." The way to develop the power is to practice every day for a few years. Many people fail and drop the practice due either to lack of time or to lack of patience. It is not easy to become an energy healer. Many are scared off when they hear that it requires practicing every day for a few years. These people don't think it worthwhile

*Figure 13   Empty force master Cai of mainland China giving a demon-
stration of adding chi to Paul Dong*

to spend this time to improve their health and attain the healing power. (If you do decide to try your hand at it, instructions are provided in Chapter 7.)

After some three years, having mastered the empty force, you will have healing power as well. At this point, you can test the strength of your healing power. The easiest way is to gather some people to test it on. Ask each one of them to hold out a hand and relax. Then, place your palm in front of each hand in turn – and send chi. After about 15 seconds, their hands should experience one of the following sensations: warmth, cold, swelling, numbness, tingling of the palm, a feeling like a cool breeze, a faint feeling like an electric current, pressure, or force. Because everyone's physique is different, reactions vary. Those who are sensitive to chi will have a strong feeling of chi flowing through the channels. Some people begin swaying. Those without sensitivity to chi will only feel warmth in the palm or have no reaction. Because of these variations in people's reactions, you must test your power on several people. Young people and females are generally most sensitive to chi and so are the most suitable subjects for testing your chi.

You may be wondering about the 15 seconds that the healing

*Figure 14    A chi kung master demonstrates the mystery of chi before a group of reporters in Beijing, China*

power takes to have an effect; for, if it were to take 15 seconds to send the empty force during a fight, wouldn't your opponent have already knocked you out? Fortunately not. When you use the empty force in a fight, you are in a state of high alertness, your spirit is forceful, and the chi you send is at its strongest. Most importantly of all, you are emitting chi with fighting intent and split-second reactions. Energy healing is different. Both you and your subject are in a state of relaxation, and your mind is working at a moderate tempo to bring good chi to the patient.

Returning to our main subject, you have to make a choice if you practice chi kung. In order to develop the empty force mainly for martial arts, you should give healings sparingly, confining them to your own family, and not releasing too much *nei chi* (internal chi). The more internal chi you give out, the weaker your empty force power will become. If you decide to go into healing, one to three healings a day are about the right number. A young healer with strong power can do as many as six healings in one day. A healing generally takes 15 to 20 minutes, or up to 30 minutes in more serious cases. No matter how serious the illness, the first healing session for a new patient should be no longer than 10 minutes. This is because some people are highly sensitive to chi and will have a strong reaction after only 10 minutes of treatment.

In ancient China, doctors or healers placed great emphasis on medical ethics. Helping people was the most important thing for them, and they didn't expect to receive high compensation. Although we now live in a money-based society, this is still the proper spirit for chi kung healing. The ethical chi kung healer, for example, first tests the chi on the patient. If the patient is not sensitive to it, the chances of a successful healing are low, and the master should explain this. Besides this, of course, the readers should bear in mind that the advice of a doctor is always recommended in case of illness, and the healer should know the limitations of chi.

For example, chi cannot help in cases of purely physical damage, such as broken limbs. Nor can it provide immediate relief from head- or stomach-aches, and it certainly cannot cure mental illness. But it can assist in treating the long-term conditions and will aid a patient's recovery and is, accordingly, most successful in the treatment of chronic health problems.

In Mainland China and some other parts of East Asia, energy healing is a fully legitimate branch of medicine. It is taught in Chinese medical schools, and chi kung masters can be found in any ordinary hospital. Unfortunately, since its validity has yet to be confirmed by Western science, it has not received comparable recognition in the West. One must respect the regional laws and regulations restricting medical practice. These regulations are based on reasonable considerations, but if a patient has a disease which is incurable by conventional methods, shouldn't acupuncture, herbal medicine, chi kung or other healing methods be allowed? The use of herbal medicine is controversial in the United States (or, of course, in Britain or Australia) because medical drugs must undergo rigorous testing before their sale can be approved by the government. Moreover, even though herbal remedies are a part of standard medical science in China, there are few doctors in the United States (and elsewhere) with the training and knowledge to use them. The use of acupuncture, however, is now licensed and legal for properly trained specialists in many American states and some other parts of the world.

We must recognize that the modern scientific mind has a tendency to reject these ancient traditions as superstitions even without a detailed study of the facts. Actually, such types of healing as energy healing or psychic healing are used all over the world. We would point out that the whole system of Chinese medicine, a highly advanced and sophisticated body of knowledge with many achievements, takes chi as a central element. Western science also has found some evidence of the effects of chi. We would hope that chi kung will gain greater acceptance in the Western world as further scientific research finds more proof for it.

## TV EXPLORES CHI

Chi kung received a boost in the West when the award-winning American journalist Bill Moyers hosted a television program called "The Mystery of Qi" as part of his series, *The Mind and Healing*, which explored the mind's role in healing. Some impressive evidence emerged. For example, one episode showed research into nerve fibers in the immune system, indicating that the brain may communicate with the immune system to affect the healing process. This research was supported by a case history in which the immune system was conditioned by psychological methods. Some Western medical researchers speculated on "the biochemistry of emotion" – the way in which emotion can be seen as both mind and matter, both psychological and material. This could constitute one of the principles of "biofeedback" in which people learn to control body processes, such as heart rate and temperature, by practicing with monitoring devices. One application of this, discussed in the program, was to train people to cure their own headaches. It seems likely that the mind influences the emotions which, in turn, may produce chemical effects on the physical condition.

This kind of hypothesis could also provide at least part of an explanation for the power of chi. In his television report, Mr. Moyers made a tour of Chinese medical facilities, guided by Dr. David Eisenburg, author of *Encounters with Qi* and the first American medical exchange student in China. His approach was a mixture of open-mindedness and skepticism. They observed Chinese herbal medicine pharmacies providing materials to be used in soup concoctions, the use of acupuncture instead of anesthesia in a brain operation, therapeutic massage, and, finally, chi kung. In a demonstration of it, Mr. Moyers himself felt his chi "moving."

Next, Mr. Moyers turned the discussion to the principles of chi kung and Chinese medicine. Instead of being based on concepts of "chemistry" or "the nervous system," as Western science dictates, it is founded on ideas such as vital energy, the balance of energies, a network of connections between various points on the body (for example, a point on the foot is associated with the liver), and health as a combination of many factors – thought, emotion, and lifestyle. The points are acupuncture points, the network is what the Chinese call meridians, and the energy flowing through the network is chi.

It is worth mentioning that the program also showed a brief demonstration of the empty force. Master Shi of Beijing used his chi to defeat several attackers. Whenever they approached him, they ended up sprawled out like marionettes on loose strings. An American student who had been living in China and studying with this master for several years tried to attack him – but couldn't make the slightest headway against him.

# COMBINING TREATMENTS TO DEFEAT DISEASE

Currently, Mainland China uses a combination of treatments for cases which can't be handled by Western medicine: energy healing, acupuncture, and herbal medicine. Excellent results have been achieved with this method, which works on the principle that, if one weapon alone isn't strong enough to win the battle against disease, one should try using three weapons. Sometimes these treatments are even combined with Western medicine.

The most widespread form of medicine in Mainland China is the combination of *wai chi* (external chi, or energy healing) with acupuncture. This is an ancient medical technique, but it had gradually passed out of use until the revival of chi kung in recent decades. According to my research, adding external chi to acupuncture not only improves its effectiveness, but can also help to correct mistakes made by an acupuncturist. For, if the needle is placed inaccurately, external chi can provide a back-up, simply because it is effective within a circle whose diameter is about an inch (2½ centimeters) – several times wider than the range of acupuncture needles. In other words, external chi provides a much wider margin of error than acupuncture treatment. Moreover, external chi enters the paths of the meridians so quickly and deeply that one treatment by chi plus acupuncture is equivalent to two treatments by acupuncture alone.

External chi can even help an acupuncturist who has chosen the wrong point altogether. This is because, no matter through which point the chi enters, it spreads throughout the entire body via the network of meridians. Thus, a number of patients have reported that chi treatment of one ailment cured another at the same time!

External chi and acupuncture have the same theoretical basis – both operate through the meridians, stimulate the chi, and regulate the chi and blood. In recent years, Chinese medical scientists have done a great deal of work on this ancient combined therapy, studying the classics and trying to improve on them, in order to revitalize a technique that was on the verge of extinction.

## HEALING: QUESTIONS AND ANSWERS

Energy healing has many applications. It plays a large part in reducing swelling, relieving inflammations, reducing tumors, destroying cancer cells, providing pain relief, and fighting rheumatism, hemiplegia, and arthritis. It works by strengthening the immune system. For treating any disease, the decisive factor is the patient's sensitivity to chi – the more sensitive, the greater the effectiveness.

In conclusion, I would like to present by way of a summary a set of questions and answers culled from many years of experience with energy healing and from the opinions of other chi kung masters.

- *What is energy healing?*
The energy is chi (vital energy). The healer sends rich internal body energy to the same points on the patient's body as are used in acupuncture.
- *Is there any pain to the patient?*
No. The healing is performed without touching and there is no pain.
- *Where does the energy come from?*
The healer has practiced chi kung daily for more than three years to develop such energy.
- *How familiar is the Western world with chi kung?*
I have taught chi kung at the San Francisco YMCA since 1985. Many major cities in the United States, Britain, and Australia, among other countries, also have such classes. In recent years, at least seven different books on chi kung have been published in the United States and England, including my own *Chi Gong: An Ancient Chinese Way to Health* (co-authored with Dr. Esser). Another, *Encounters with Qi*, was written by an American doctor, David Eisenburg. (See also the Bibliography at the back of this book.)
- *Is this like psychic healing?*
No. Psychic "energy" may not always be present, but trained chi energies always are.
- *How does the healing act on the patient?*
The energy is guided by the mind from the center of the palm or finger and directed at the acupuncture points on the patient's body. The energy can also be transmitted to a needle for combined chi kung-acupuncture healing.

● *What kinds of diseases does it heal?*
Illnesses of the nervous system, pains, and most chronic diseases.
● *Does this healing have any harmful effects on the patient?*
No. The healing is without touch and no medicine is given. All the patient has to do is to relax. Human body energy used in this way never harms anyone.
● *How does it cure diseases?*
According to Chinese medical theory, some people become sick because their energy is becoming weak or their meridians (energy flow channels) are blocked. The internal systems then lose their functions, causing the body to become "out of balance." When the healer regenerates the patient's energy, the body's systems regain their functions. Vital energy stimulates the meridians, vivifies the nervous system, and promotes the blood circulation – all of which helps strengthen immunity to diseases.
● *Is this kind of healing good for mental diseases?*
No. There are no cases to show that energy healing can help mental diseases.
● *How often should energy healing be applied?*
Usually, every day or every other day, depending on the severity of the disease. One healing takes 10 or 20 minutes, or up to 30 minutes for serious cases. The first time, the healing should be tried for a maximum of 10 minutes, because some people are extremely sensitive to chi and may react too strongly.
● *Which people are particularly sensitive to chi?*
This can only be determined by testing. A subject extends a hand and relaxes. The healer then sends chi to the subject's palm. After a short time, he will determine the subject's feelings of warmth, cold, numbness, swelling, tingling, pressure, or something like an electric flow. If the subject experiences strong sensations, he or she is sensitive to chi. One who is particularly sensitive to chi may lose control and start moving around, or may feel chi flowing throughout the body. One who is not sensitive to chi will feel nothing.
● *Is chi treatment effective on people with no sensitivity to chi?*
The effects will be much weaker, with some exceptions. Chinese medical evidence shows that five percent of those not sensitive to chi will still be cured. The reason is unknown.
● *Are there different levels of sensitivity to chi?*
Yes. They can be roughly divided into four classes: highly sensitive, sensitive, somewhat sensitive, and not sensitive.

● *What are the effects of combining chi kung with acupuncture?*
Of course the effects are stronger when the two are combined.
This requires the cooperation of a chi kung master and an
acupuncturist, or a person who has both chi kung and acupuncture abilities. This method is generally used in cases which can't
be cured by acupuncture alone.

● *Are there any special benefits of energy healing?*
Yes. For example, if you come for a healing for your headache,
the energy healing may cure other problems at the same time.
When the chi enters the acupuncture points, it circulates throughout the body and has beneficial effects on all areas.

● *How convenient is energy healing?*
It is simple and convenient. It does not require any facilities or
medical instruments, and it can be done anywhere.

# Chapter Seven

# A "How-To" Guide to the Empty Force

Blue dye comes from the indigo plant, but is bluer;
Ice comes from water, but is colder

The above couplet, from the ancient Chinese classic *Xunzi Quan Xue* (Xunzi's Encouragement of Study), means that students become more skilled than their teachers. I have put it at the start of this chapter to encourage all empty force students and to wish them success in surpassing their teachers, just as blue coloring surpasses the indigo plant and ice surpasses water.

It should be stressed at this stage that the empty force is the outcome of a discipline that is as much spiritual as physical. Purity of intention is paramount, and any power acquired should never be misused for self-serving ends nor to damage others except, in cases of dire need, for self-defense.

As its name implies, the empty force produces its effects without physical contact. We know that an electric current is transmitted through wire, but electromagnetism does not require any such physical link to attract iron. In the same way, the empty force doesn't require any contact with the hands or the body to produce its effects. People imagine that this technique must be very difficult to learn but, in fact, another technique which comes from yi quan and which *does* require physical contact – is harder, and fewer people can master it. The reason will be explained below.

Sometimes, the moment for action is more important than whether or not physical contact is involved. A power that normally requires physical contact can work without contact when a practitioner is taken by surprise and the empty force is, as it were, emitted spontaneously. At the highest level of yi quan

71

mastery, for instance, at the instant one intuits a sneak attack, the jing explodes, manifesting as the empty force, without the need for any physical contact.

## UNRAVELING SOME AREAS OF CONFUSION

Before we look at empty force exercises in detail, we need to clear up a couple of potential areas of confusion. Why do some people seem to use the empty force, but deny it? And why are there different kinds of empty force? Interestingly, most of Wang Xiangzhai's students deny that the power they use is the empty force, claiming instead that it is simply the jing developed in the course of yi quan, a force which does usually require physical contact. The reasons for this are most likely the following: Wang lived in the conservative era of the 1930s, when people were loath to believe in any ability to knock people down without physical contact. At best, people would take it with a grain of salt. So, even if he really could knock people down in this way, Wang wouldn't have wanted to admit it. He would have been accused of making an unscientific claim or of self-delusion, as in the example of Yue Huanzhi (see p. 33).

Previously, I have also mentioned an empty force master living in Berkeley, California who cautions his students not to promote the empty force to British or Americans, because they wouldn't believe it and this would have a negative effect on his reputation. What he says is quite correct. If you describe the empty force to 100 British or Americans, probably only one would believe it, one with a curious mind. Another reason is that – since their power is developed over five or six years of rigorous practice, several hours a day – yi quan practitioners can always defeat an opponent with physical contact, so why should they be interested in a force whose reality is greeted with extreme skepticism?

It is sometimes difficult for people to put the truth above their own career prospects, as the example of an expert from Harvard Medical School shows. He went to Mainland China to investigate chi kung and made his own observations of its use in the treatment of cancer. But when he returned, he never said a word about using chi kung to treat cancer, maintaining instead that chi kung is no more than a relaxation response. Having spent his whole life in attaining his valuable position in the medical profession, he found himself unable to put it in jeopardy just to promote Chinese chi kung.

This reminds me of another example. Several years ago, some researchers at China's Beijing Observatory discovered convincing evidence that the first discoverer of the satellites of Jupiter was not Galileo but an ancient Chinese astronomer, Gan De, who lived two thousand years before Galileo. I sent an article about this ("Did Galileo Discover the Satellites of Jupiter?") to British, American, and German scientific journals, but they ignored it. Nobody wanted to revise Galileo's established reputation. People, it seems, are too often more concerned to uphold the established order than to acknowledge the truth.

Unfortunately, the conditions under which yi quan can lead to the empty force have not been seriously investigated. For example, yi quan can produce an explosive power in moments of dire need. Moreover, sometimes the empty force comes about in a border zone between physical contact and no contact. An experienced empty force master would say this kind of jing comes from shi jing (solid force) and kong jing (empty force), rather like chemical change which can be viewed either as "energy fluctuation" or as "energy transformation" regardless of where this energy came from. These three varieties of the empty force all come from standing-on-stake; and since this is the key to the empty force, it is hardly surprising if yi quan, which derives from the same source, can under certain circumstances produce the same effect. So, perhaps we do not really need to distinguish too exactly between physical and non-physical contact.

The above three kinds of empty force can be categorized as martial arts empty force, or *ling kong jing* in Chinese. Another kind of empty force, used for healing, is a soft energy or force. Because it follows different procedures and methods of practice, it produces different effects and has different strengths and weaknesses. This soft empty force is called kong jing in Chinese. Non-Chinese speaking students often confuse the two and purchase the wrong kind of empty force video tape. (It might advertise itself as an "empty force" tape, but is actually about kong jing, not ling kong jing.) So, be warned!

# PREPARING TO PRACTICE THE EMPTY FORCE

This chapter concerns three kinds of empty force and their techniques. But first of all, I must explain four key factors.

1 All physical exercises, including tai chi and martial arts, emphasize *motion*, but the empty force emphasizes *stillness*.

2 All chi kung, tai chi, and martial arts exercises should be practiced *outdoors*, particularly by trees, lakes, or rivers, but the empty force should be practiced *indoors*. If the indoor space is too wide and open, the doors and windows should be closed. This is one of the secrets of practicing internal arts. Outdoors, chi and energy are easily dissipated, but indoors they remain concentrated and, as the months pass, the space will be organized into a "chi field." This energy field will be good for the growth and health of the power.

3 Ninety-five percent of the power of the empty force comes from standing-on-stake. How well you stand, and how long you spend standing, affect the level of power you will attain. Standing-on-stake is an exercise in stillness.

4 Other martial arts also make use of standing-on-stake as one of the main practices, so why is the empty force so much more powerful? In my opinion, there are two reasons. First, the standing-on-stake practice in martial arts doesn't last as long. It usually involves three to six months' practice of 15 minutes to half an hour a day. For the empty force, practice starts at 10 minutes a day, adding five minutes to this every week until it reaches an hour or more; nor does the practice stop after three or six months. Second, and more important, is that martial arts standing-on-stake practice uses strength, but the empty force is just the opposite – it uses relaxation. Training with the strength is an external practice, but training with relaxation is an internal practice. The former develops the arms, legs, and muscles, but the latter develops *nei jing* (internal jing, or force). This book has had much to say about jing, and all jing comes from standing-on-stake.

Why is stillness stronger than motion? This seemingly contradictory idea was suggested by long observation of trees. A tree stands upright, never moving, but inside it is in constant motion. A great tree standing on the ground, towering over all things, is an image of strength. After mastering the empty force, you will be like a great tree looking down silently from a position of strength.

Now we are in a position to explain how to practice the empty force. First, we must do some preparations for the practice. Have a light snack or a cup of warm soup or milk (this may be skipped when you don't feel hungry). However, it is important to avoid having a full stomach. Go to the bathroom beforehand. Wear loose clothing. Maintain a cheerful mood – it is better to avoid practicing in a bad mood. Do not consume any liquor within an hour before or after practicing. Choose a quiet place; practice there every day. As explained above, this will help your energy to become concentrated in one spot.

Wear the same clothes. (I recommend choosing two sets, one for summer and one for winter.) Gradually, over the months and years of practice, the clothes will become "energy clothes," a precious asset the quality of which money can't buy. This not only brings health benefits, but also preserves your power. Believe it or not, it can even have healing powers. If someone has a mild disease (a common cold, headache, or discomfort), he or she will recover faster by wearing the energy clothes.

Do not engage in sexual activity within an hour before or after practicing. Also, reduce sexual activity as much as possible in the first three months of the practice. Chinese traditional thinking maintains that frequent sexual activity weakens the power. Western readers may not agree with this, but I present it for your information.

Finally, practitioners should be between the ages of 15 and 50. (The upper limit can be raised to 55 for those in fit condition.) This is a fighting chi kung practice, not a health promotion chi kung practice, so it is unsuitable for people in fragile health. The most important thing is to obtain the approval of your family doctor for you to do this practice.

In the following section, I shall introduce three empty force practices. It is extremely important not to mix them up or try to practice more than one at the same time. Unfocused practice is sure to fail. However, you can try them all out first by doing each practice for one month and then selecting the one you prefer. After that, you should only do that one practice.

## EMPTY FORCE A

**Part One**

*Warm-up Exercise*

First do half an hour of tai chi movements. There are many forms of tai chi, such as Yang style, Chen style, Sun style, Wu style, and so on. The best choices are Yang style and Chen style. Since this is a book on the empty force, we will not go into details on how to practice tai chi. The Bibliography at the back of this book gives information on relevant reading. Besides, tai chi has become more popular than martial arts these days, and one can find classes in most cities, many of them free of charge. At the same time, tai chi involves many movements which are hard to describe in words, and even harder to follow. As the experience of many people has proven, it is difficult to become good at tai chi even by studying a video.

It is not essential to know tai chi in order to warm up – any soft exercise, such as dancing, will do instead. But it ought to be noted that a knowledge of tai chi is not only helpful but highly desirable for attaining the more advanced levels of the empty force.

**Part Two**

*Push Hands Exercise*

1 Stand upright in a natural posture.
2 Turn your right foot about 35 degrees to the right.
3 Move your left foot one step forward. Bend your legs slightly, keeping the eyes open.
4 Starting in front of the chest, push your hands forward and circle them back around. The left hand moves around and back to the left side, and the right hand back to the right, until the hands meet again in front of the chest. Do this 12 times. After one month of practice, increase it to 24 times, and by the third month increase it to 36 times. From then on, keep doing it 36 times.
5 Pull your left foot back to the normal position, and return the right foot to its normal position. Straighten the legs.

6 Stand upright in a natural posture.
7 Turn your left foot about 35 degrees to the left.
8 Put your right foot one step forward.
9 Push your hands around and back to the chest 12 times. This time, the circles go in the opposite direction. Increase the number of circles month-by-month to 36 times, as before.

When doing push hands exercises, be sure to concentrate on the palms and imagine that your palms are touching something such as water, sand, grass, etc. (*see* Figure 15, p. 78).


## Part Three – A

*Standing-on-Stake Exercise*

1 Stand upright.
2 Move your left foot to the left, such that the feet are about a shoulder-width apart.
3 Relax, empty your mind, and close your eyes.
4 Concentrate on your hands and imagine your hands getting light and floating up slowly, palms down, then bend your legs slightly. (*See* Figure 15.) Imagine the chi (energy) coming from the sky and filling your body; then concentrate on the whole body or on natural scenes like oceans, mountains, the cosmos, etc. Begin practicing this posture ten minutes a day for the first week, then add five minutes each week up to a total of 30 minutes.
5 Practice the above posture for three months, then add a new posture to practice after this: raise your hands from posture one to your forehead (*see* Figure 16) and continue your standing-on-stake practice. Practice this posture five minutes a day for the first week, and add five minutes each week up to 30 minutes. Now the total time including both postures is one hour.

Practice the above for one year, then add the following.


## Part Three – B

*Projecting the Chi (Energy)*

6 Drop your hands on both the left and right hand sides. Concentrate on the fingers (both sides) for five minutes. Imagine

*Figure 15   Posture one of standing-on-stake*

your fingers have a lot of chi, and move your arms up and down alternately, left arm first, fingers pointing to the ground. Imagine your fingers are shooting chi bullets into the ground (*see* Figure 17), and project your chi into the ground three feet down or deep into the earth. Practice each side 12 times.

7 Raise your hands to the sky with the fingers pointing up and palms facing each other. Concentrate on your fingers for a little while and then bend your legs a little more and project the chi to the sky. Raise and lower the arms alternately, starting with the left arm. Imagine the chi flowing into the distance. Do this six times on each side.

8 Lower your hands to the chest area and turn your body and arms to the left, your left hand in front of your right, and stand motionlessly. Project the chi from your fingers ahead

*Figure 16    Posture two of standing-on-stake*

*Figure 17    A posture for projecting chi into the ground*

*Figure 18   Projecting the chi from the fingers*

and into the distance as in Figure 18. Then turn the body and arms to the right and practice the same thing, right hand in front of left. Practice this 12 seconds for each side.

### Practice in Leading the Chi to a Dummy

9 Hang a dummy or a picture in front of you, at a distance of about ten feet. Concentrate on its feet for a while and focus your mind, eyes and fingers to guide the chi from your toes straight to its toes and up to its chest. Swoop down with your arms as if scooping the chi from your feet toward the dummy. Concentrate the mind strongly on making the dummy fall backward.

### Silent Sitting Meditation

10 Sit in a comfortable chair, about a third of the way in, without leaning on the back. Place the legs about a shoulder-width apart. Drop your hands beside your body. Relax and close your eyes. Imagine that the chi is coming from the sky and filling your body. Now concentrate on the whole body or

on nature scenes (ocean, mountains, cosmos, etc.) Practice this meditation for 30 minutes and add five minutes each week until the total reaches one hour or more.

**Part Four**

*Ending Exercise*

1 Tell yourself that you are going to end the exercise. Then open your eyes and stand up.
2 Take three deep breaths. With each breath, circle the arms up and around, raising the hands (palms up) when you breathe in, and dropping your hands (palms down) when you breathe out.
3 Rub both hands together in front of your chest until they become warm, then wipe your hands all over your face a few times.
4 Use your right hand to pat your left arm from the shoulder to the hand a few times, and your left hand to pat your right arm.
5 Bending over, pat your legs a few times from top to bottom, using your right hand for the right leg and your left hand for the left. Then straighten up your body.

*Note*: it is very important to do the ending exercise after the practice.

**Extra practice (to begin after two years)**

*Alert Posture Practice*

1 Stand upright in a natural posture.
2 Turn your right foot about 45 degrees to the right.
3 Move your left foot about one step forward, bend your legs and raise your hands up to the chest area, left hand in front of right. This posture (*see* Figure 19) is performed facing to the left.
4 Stand upright in a natural posture.
5 Turn your left foot about 45 degrees to the left.
6 Move your right foot about one step forward, bend your legs and raise your hands up to the chest area, right hand in front of left. This posture is performed facing to the right.

*Figure 19   An alert posture*

Practice this alert posture for a maximum of five minutes in each direction, two or three times a day. During this exercise, you should be highly alert, as if facing a tiger and ready to fight.

*Energy Penetration (following alert posture practice)*

Stand about 10–12 feet (3 meters) away from a dummy or a big tree, focus your mind and spirit, and then look at it very hard. At that moment, send out all of your energy to penetrate the dummy. It is essential that you believe you can do it. If you can penetrate the dummy, you can easily penetrate the human body. Practice this for half a minute. Next, concentrate the spirit and loudly shout "Hey" (or whatever you usually shout at people), at the same time putting out both arms to send the empty force toward the dummy. The sound of the voice combined with the empty force is designed to knock down the target.

Strong chi can penetrate all kinds of materials, but do not try to penetrate aluminum or a mirror. You might sustain an injury because they reflect the energy.

   The following factors determine one's success in acquiring the empty force:

- Practice every day except when sick.
- Practice for more than three years.
- Specialize in one kind of empty force.
- Maintain a happy spirit, free from emotional problems in your marriage, family or workplace.
- Maintain confidence in the practice.
- In the first three years, preserve abundant energy. Don't give healings or demonstrations, because these will decrease the energy.

After mastering this practice, your empty force will knock down anyone sensitive to chi (about six out of every ten people). Those who are not knocked down will suffer a greater misfortune, because they will be injured more seriously than those sensitive to chi.

## EMPTY FORCE B (EMPTY FORCE FROM THE FINGERS)

### Part One

The procedure is the same as for Empty Force A. Follow the instructions for push hands in exactly the same way, except that you should concentrate on the fingers, especially the index and middle finger, rather than the palms of the hands.

Similarly, follow the instructions for standing-on-stake, except that, having imagined the chi filling your whole body in step four, mentally concentrate it into the fingers. At step *five*, begin a new practice for the index and middle fingers, thus:

5 Light an ordinary long candle. Put it on a table or shelf about 5–6 inches (12–15 centimeters) away, at a height of somewhere between the chest and the shoulder.
6 Stand upright in a natural posture, facing the candle.
7 Put your left foot to the left, about a shoulder width apart from the right.
8 Take one step forward with your right foot. Bend your legs slightly and keep your eyes open.
9 Place the left hand on the hip, and the right hand on the side of, and slightly above, the chest, with the right index finger and middle finger together (called "sword finger" in martial arts).

*Figure 20   A group of students practising the Empty Force B with a candle on the table*

10 Focusing the mind with strong intention, point your sword finger at the candle flame. Use the mind to guide the chi energy from the sword finger to the candle. Practice this exercise for five minutes a day; then, each week, add five minutes to the daily exercise until it reaches 20 or 30 minutes. Practice should take place between 4:00 and 5:00 a.m. and 11:00 and 12:00 midnight, and should continue until you can make the candle flicker and, finally, go out. Do this practice indoors.

**Part Two**

1 Make a cotton ball about the size of a ping-pong ball and hang it in your room by a fine thread. Close the windows and doors.
2 Stand upright in a natural posture, bend the legs slightly, and face the cotton ball.
3 Point at the target with the sword finger, holding the fingers very close to, but not touching, the cotton ball. Focus the intention, as if pushing yourself strongly toward the cotton ball. Do this practice twice a day for five minutes, once in the morning and once at night. The exact time doesn't matter, but the two practice sessions should be at least four hours apart. Do this until you can move the cotton ball. Then, stand

slightly farther from the cotton ball. Gradually practice from farther and farther away. Stop when you reach a distance of 8–10 feet (2–3 meters).

4 Replace the cotton ball with a ball made of half cotton and half cloth, or something heavier than a cotton ball. Practice in the same manner until your pointing can move the ball at about 8–10 feet (2–3 meters).

5 Now use a heavier object, such as a cloth ball, and practice the same thing.

**Part Three**

1 Light a candle in the room, but this time put a thin piece of paper between you and it.

2 Stand upright in a natural posture, bend the legs slightly, and face the candle which should be placed four to five feet away (about one-and-a-half meters).

3 Point with the finger as described above. Since the flame is blocked by paper, the power cannot immediately penetrate it. However, gradually, it will be able to penetrate, like a light breeze, and make the flame waver – slightly at first and then violently. The flame will bob up and down and be on the verge of burning out. Finally, it will be put out completely. It takes at least half a year or so to achieve this power.

4 Replace the paper with a thicker paper and practice in the same way.

5 After succeeding with the above, use a piece of cloth instead of paper to block the candle and practice in the same way. Gradually increase the distance, until it reaches about six feet.

*Note*: After the exercises given in Parts One to Three, massage the fingers after finishing the practice (because the fingers will be tired), and then do silent sitting meditation for 30 to 60 minutes.

Whereas Empty Force A sends chi from the palms, this Finger Empty Force sends chi from the fingers. The latter focuses on a smaller area, is more powerful and more flexible, but is harder to master than Empty Force A.

For both Empty Force A and B, you must obtain the approval of your physician and physical training specialist before undertaking the practice.

# EMPTY FORCE C

## Part One

Similar to yi quan, this technique can be practiced indoors or outdoors, as follows:

1 Rise at dawn every morning. After washing your face, do confidence-building practice in front of a mirror. Imagine you are the strongest person in the world, with the ability to knock down any opponent, no matter how powerful. Survey the world with supreme confidence.
2 Practice Yang-style tai chi for half an hour per day, gradually increasing it to 45 minutes or more.
3 Do a push hands exercise as described earlier in Empty Force A or B. Take a little break.

## Part Two

*Standing-on-Stake Exercise*

1 Stand upright, eyes open and looking straight ahead or into the distance at hills, forests and rivers.
2 Move your left foot about a shoulder-width to the left, with both feet rooted to the ground like a tree, toes clenched down, and head upright.
3 Relax and empty your mind.
4 Bend your legs slightly. Slowly raise your hands level with the stomach, positioning the arms as if they were holding a large ball. This is posture one (*see* Figure 21). Practice this three times a day for five minutes at a time, raising it to ten minutes after a month.
5 After completing the practice for posture one, raise the arms up to the chest area, palms facing the chest. This is posture two (*see* Figure 22). Again, imagine you are holding a ball in your arms. Practice this three times a day for five minutes each time, and raise it to ten minutes each time after a month.
6 After completing posture two, raise the hands up to head level, palms facing the forehead (refer back to Figure 16, p. 79). This is posture three. Practice this three times a day for five minutes at a time, raising it to ten minutes after a month.

*Figure 21    Posture one*

*Figure 22    Posture two*

*Figure 23   Posture four (also called the "little step posture")*

*Figure 24   Posture five (also called "big step posture" or "tiger con-
trolling posture")*

7 Stand upright, move your left foot about a shoulder-width to the left and half a step forward. Bend the legs and shift the body weight back. The sole of the foot should be slightly raised, and the knee sticking out. The body weight is distributed about 60 per cent on the back foot and 40 percent on the front. The hands are raised to shoulder-level, elbows bent in an embrace position, palms inward, fingers spread apart, eyes looking straight ahead. This is posture four (also called "little step posture") and it is shown in Figure 23.

8 Stand upright and move your left foot to the left *more than a shoulder width*. Move your left foot half a step forward, bend both legs, and distribute your weight about 40 percent forward and 60 percent back. The hands are above the knees, and the arms are in a grasping position as if holding down a tiger (*see* Figure 24). This is posture five, also called the "big step posture" or the "tiger-controlling posture." Practice this posture as a continuation of posture four three times a day, three minutes each time.

9 Practice the alert posture – this is posture six (*see* Figure 19, p. 82) – for 1 to 2 minutes, as instructed in the Extra Practice section of Empty Force A. Practice this posture twice a day, as a continuation of posture five.

Practice all of the above postures for a year. Then, you can vary the order of the postures (but the alert posture must always be practiced last). Practice the combined postures in free order for 45 minutes or more, once a day.

10 Now, you can add posture seven to replace posture one (i.e. step 4). This posture is similar to the little step posture (Figure 23) but without raising the soles of the feet. Change the hand positions, as in Figure 25.

11 Add posture eight to replace posture two (i.e. step 5). Everything is the same except the head is swivelled to the left or to the right alternately, as in Figure 26.

12 Add posture nine, with the arms facing out on both sides, as in Figure 27.

13 Add posture ten as in Figure 28, with the hands up, elbows bent, palms facing outward, and knees slightly bent.

Practice the earlier postures (i.e. steps 1–9) combined with the more advanced postures (i.e. steps 10–13) for another year.

*Figure 25    Posture seven*

*Figure 26    Posture eight*

*Figure 27    Posture nine*

*Figure 28    Posture ten*

**Part Three**

*Muscle-Stretching Practice*

Muscle-stretching practice starts with the third year of the practice. You can select any posture for this practice (except postures 4, 5 and 6). After doing standing-on-stake for one minute, use the mind to move the flexors and extensors of the arms and legs. The purpose is to strengthen these muscle systems, increase their flexibility and mobility, and to link the limbs together into a single system.

First, we must understand that there are three types of muscle: smooth, myocardial, and striated. Their location and features are as follows:

- *Smooth muscle*: The muscles of the stomach, intestines, bladder, uterus and the walls of the blood vessels. Their contraction is slow and long-lasting.
- *Myocardial muscle*: The muscles of the heart. Their contractions are faster than the smooth muscles and are coordinated.
- *Striated muscle*: Mostly attached to the skeleton, and therefore also called skeletal muscle. These include muscles of the head, torso, arms and legs. They contract quickly and powerfully, but are easily fatigued. They can be contracted at will, so they can be contracted and released by turns.

The two groups of skeletal muscles are distributed on either side of an axis of motion and they function in opposite ways – one consists of the flexors, situated on the side of a joint bending in, such as the palm side of the hand; the other refers to the extensors, situated on the outer, extending side of the joint. Although these muscles function in opposition to each other, they are interdependent. When a joint is bent, the flexor is working and the extensor is at rest. Conversely, when the extensor is working, the flexor rests. Both contract alternately, and they cannot contract at the same time.

Now, do some mind-directed exercises to contract the muscles of the limbs (especially the finger muscles). This is to train the body to become a more unified system. The training method is to *maintain the standing-on-stake posture while using the mind to stretch the muscles*. Since the mind controls this exercise, it must be done when in a state of spiritual contentment. It can only work if distracting thoughts are eliminated and the spirit is united. This training should not exceed 15 minutes, and should be abandoned when the mind becomes tired.

The muscle-stretching exercise is started by using the mind to contract and release the flexor, so it is also called the loosening and tightening exercise. If you persist in this exercise every day, the muscles will build toughness and endurance. The next step is to link the muscles of the different limbs. Your arm and leg muscles will become like a rubber band – tough, durable and powerful. The linking method is to "pull" forcibly at both ends of the limb, or to "pull" at one end while "holding" the other end steady, tensing and relaxing in turn. The point of this is to organize the flexor muscles of every joint of every limb into a unit. It begins with the feet, then moves to the shank, thigh, buttocks, stomach (do not practice this with a full stomach), back, arms, and head. When all the muscles in the body are working together, you gain more power and can beat an opponent stronger than yourself. (At this point I am filled with admiration for the foresight of the inventors of yi quan. After we understand these training methods, we come to believe in what was previously unbelievable – the source of yi quan's fierce power. However, such a complex and demanding technique is not suitable for self-instruction, and should be done under a master's supervision.)

The arms are very important in muscle-stretching practice. All the joints from the wrists to the shoulder should be stretched and linked. The last are the palms and the fingers which, like an automobile's bumper, bear the brunt of the opponent's force and carry your own force. They must be trained in the same way. One year of this practice can be seen as basic training, two years' practice improves the quality, and three years' allow you to face a strong opponent.

## Training for Winning Through Mind Power

After three years of practice, you should begin a special training called "training for winning through mind power." This is a higher-level mental activity requiring the uniting of all the flexor muscles of the limbs, before "expanding the spirit," as it is called, and extending its force to make a connection with a target outside the body.

First, practice with a large tree in front of you. Expand your spirit and extend its strength so that it feels as if the fingers of both your hands are connecting with the tree trunk. Visualize your arms grabbing the trunk and slowly pulling it toward you, then pushing it back. Repeat this practice over and over, for the purpose of gaining control over the target and achieving a state in which your power penetrates, suffuses, and controls your opponent. In actual combat situations, this will give you a strategic advantage. Before the enemy goes into action, your power has already gone through him, assuring your victory.

**Supplementary Exercises**

After mastering all of the above exercises, you still may have some deficiencies. These will probably lie in foot strength, balance, and voice power, and are remedied in the following ways:

*Training Foot Strength for Advance and Retreat*

Stand in the push hands exercise posture, with the toes clenched, starting with the left foot forward. Lean the body forward, and raise the hands to chest level in the same way as before, but do not move. This practice is only for training the feet to bear the brunt of this movement. When the body is leaning forward, the center of gravity and the attention are focused on the left foot, and when the body moves back, they are focused on the right foot. Do this 36 times, then switch the roles of the feet and do it another 36 times.

*Training Foot Strength for Left and Right Leaning*

Stand in the "big step posture," with the toes clenched and the hands raised to chest level, as above. Starting with the left side, lean the body to the left. Now the left foot carries the weight, and the center of gravity and attention are concentrated on the left foot. Next, lean the body to the right, and train the right foot to carry the weight, as before. Do this exercise 36 times for both sides.

*Balance Training*

There are two reasons for practicing physical balance. The first is to strengthen the feet, and the second is to prepare for the need to maintain balance when the feet bear the brunt of an opponent's attack – you must avoid letting the body's center of gravity shift to the side or sink down. The method is as follows: stand upright with the feet together, the toes clenched, and the arms spread open like a bird's wings. Bend both legs, knees outside the toes, with the center of gravity firmly on the right foot. Raise the left foot one or two inches in the air and swing it half a step forward. Then, move it a full step to the left, completing an arc with the foot. These two motions should flow smoothly, with the foot one or two inches off the ground. Next, shifting the center of gravity to the left foot, the right foot goes half a step forward, completes a step toward the left foot without touching the ground, and is again placed next to the left foot. Proceeding forward in this way, take 12 steps, ending with the right foot. When the two feet are together again, do the same motions going backwards, with the left foot stepping back first.

### Voice Response Training

As mentioned earlier, Chen Gong's *Taiji Quan Pu* has a section which says (in paraphrase) that the empty force is very mysterious, almost mystical, and if a strong master loudly shouts "Ha!" the target will lose the power to resist, or may even be knocked down. In this section, we turn to the study of this mystery.

This training should be done at dawn. It is best done in the hills. At the first crack of dawn, take a breath of air from the direction of the sun, and visualize yourself absorbing the sun's first chi, becoming filled with energy and vigor. Then, loudly shout "Ha!" and visualize with confident belief that an opponent standing before you will be knocked down. This imaginary opponent must fall when hit with your three years' worth of empty force practice, using the combined might of five kinds of power – jing power, mind power, spiritual power, eye power, and voice power.

### Daily Silent Sitting Meditation Practice

When you start practicing Empty Force C, you must do daily meditation practice for 45 minutes to an hour. The methods are the same as described earlier. It is fine to use either the lotus position or to sit in a chair. The most important thing is to do it

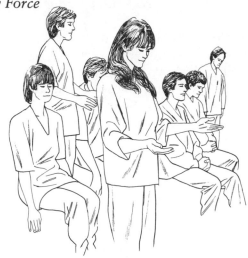

*Figure 29    A group of students doing silent sitting meditation. Some students are standing up because the chi automatically pulls them up*

every day without fail and without interruption. Standing-on-stake is the source of strength, while meditation is to concentrate the strength you have developed and preserve it. For this reason, both standing-on-stake and meditation are indispensable. However, standing-on-stake must be done before meditation, and the ending exercise must be done after the meditation.

## THE TIME PROBLEM

By now you must have noticed the time problem in all of these practices. A glance through them shows that they require at least three hours a day. This is impractical for most urban dwellers, and even more so for anyone who is married with children. Not only do you need a doctor's approval, you must also seek understanding from your spouse and children. Otherwise, you may be forced to give up the practice. Most Chinese who master the empty force come from the countryside or mountain areas. Some are monks or Taoist priests who have renounced the world and become one with nature. Finally, this practice is very difficult and for the best chance of success it should be done under the supervision of a master.

Chapter Eight

# The Students Speak: Experiences with the Empty Force and Chi Kung

This chapter takes a creative approach. I deeply believe that a book on martial arts or chi kung will be improved by including the personal experiences and opinions of students of the art (especially the author's students), or other colleagues and specialists in the area. I feel this makes it more interesting and broadens the perspective. Below I present the experiences of several students and colleagues along with brief biographical sketches and information on how to contact them in case the reader wants to learn more.

## AN ACUPUNCTURIST LEARNS EMPTY FORCE FOR HEALING
by Karen Cameron, Dipl. Ac., M.S.

"I can knock you over with just my chi," he said. It wasn't a challenge to fight, nor was it directed to one person alone, but rather a simple statement of truth as he saw it, and directed to all of us – "us" being a class of first-day chi kung students at San Francisco College of Acupuncture; "he" being Paul Dong, teacher and chi kung master. We giggled a little nervously, looking to each other for a way to interpret his remarkable statement. Could he really do it? Knock us over without touching us? This small, lightweight, middle-aged, smiling man who potentially held mysterious powers? The males of the class were beginning to swagger a bit. "No way, man!" I could imagine them thinking.

They were decades younger, each a good foot taller, more muscular, heavier by far, and in their minds, no doubt, no pushovers. The females just tittered a bit more, and looked back at the source of this intriguing idea – knock us over indeed!

But Paul continued to smile with confidence. He quietly lined us up into two queues of 15 each, having us stand with our toes and chins nearly touching the class member in front of us. We waited expectantly. "Don't try to resist," he cautioned, "but close your eyes and let the chi move through you."

I thought about my textbook encounters with chi, and wondered idly if any of the definitions I had read fitted the occasion. One text said that "chi" was impossible to translate because no one word could approximate its essence exactly, but it could be variously rendered as "energy, material force, matter, ether, matter-energy, vital force, life force, vital power, and moving power." Furthermore, the text continued, "the reason it is so difficult to translate the word qi [chi] correctly lies precisely in its fluid nature whereby qi can assume different manifestations and be different things in different situations . . . Qi is at the basis of all phenomena in the universe and provides a continuity between coarse, material forms and tenuous, rarefied, non-material energies."[1] So what was about to happen here with chi as empty force?

By this time Paul was admonishing us again to stand in a straight line and to close our eyes. My last glimpse of him informed me that he had taken a target-shooting stance about five feet from us, with legs bent and knees apart, arms outstretched and pointing toward the first person in our group. I was third in line. Not knowing quite what to expect, I stood patiently. Should I dig my feet into the ground? Brace myself a bit more? Would I feel anything? Would I – My thoughts were interrupted by the swaying of the girl in front of me. She had begun to back up. I too felt the wave of gentle force at about the same time. My upper body seemed to be moving backward while my feet struggled to stay put. It was like dominoes from then on: all fifteen of us found ourselves backing up and staggering to keep our balance. The other group began to laugh in earnest. How silly we looked! We joined in the laughter, somewhat bewildered by what had just occurred. The force was so subtle, and yet so insistent – we *had* to move!

The other group fared no better than we in standing their

ground. I thoroughly enjoyed watching them tottering, to their own astonishment. Amazing, I thought; how'd he do it?

But the show wasn't over yet. Paul directed the biggest, tallest, strongest-looking male student to stand in front of the classroom door, while he went to the other side, closed the door, and projected his chi through it to the student, with the intent once more of knocking him over. The student took his place with some self-conscious grinning, and assumed his stance with the bravado of a football offensive lineman defending his quarterback. No dice – within moments, he too was swaying slightly back and forth, then more obviously, to be finally knocked off his feet. He had backed up halfway across the room! So much for brute strength. Paul definitely had our attention then. We had all been subjected to, and had witnessed, the powers of empty force; it was an experience I'll never forget.

Although the course that spring of 1991 at the Acupuncture College was designed not only to introduce us to chi kung but also to be an intensive practice for learning to build up our chi and then releasing it externally for healing, the focus was not on empty force per se. However, we did learn to feel the chi within us, to move it around our own body internally, and to direct it out of our fingertips to another person, directly or via acupuncture needles.

We compared the sensations that student volunteers received from acupuncture alone to those of acupuncture with chi kung directed into the needles. Big difference! The *de chi* ("arrival of chi") sensations of soreness, tingling, distension, or heaviness were much more pronounced. Even without the needles, *de chi* could be effective: one advanced chi kung student pointed his index finger a few inches away from ST36 (*zu san li* acupuncture point) just below my right knee, and fired away. I felt the activation of chi there immediately and its movement down the front of my leg to the tip of my second toe. That was quite amazing to me – actually to feel the course of the stomach channel internally, as well as to know its pathway intellectually.

I suspect that the mapping out of acupuncture channels in ancient times occurred in a similar way, that is, via sensitive individuals who, through meditation or visualization, had learned to observe, develop, and move their chi within. They then began to take notice of how it circulated in their bodies and kept records. They then compared their notes with others who were doing it too, and the pathways were inscribed on human figurines for the benefit of posterity. Individual points could have been designated after the channels had been mapped or, as some think, concurrently – by "happy accidents" when a body injury in a specific area produced a beneficial result locally or somewhere else on the body. No doubt they noticed that these "points" were located along the lines of chi flow. Pricking, massaging, or pressing them released the pain caused by the obstruction of chi, or a "traffic jam," if you will.

I experienced a real snarl of a traffic jam myself (not on the freeway, but in class) when Paul demonstrated his empty force again one day for visitors. We students lined up as we had before and quietly awaited the subtle flow of energy which we knew would gently rock us over. This time, however, was different. Unwittingly I was wearing a quarter-sized amethyst pendant which hung down midway between my breasts. I didn't realize then that this was to be the target area for Paul's directed energy. The crystal stone must have magnified the force, for I was certainly knocked over, and experienced a tight chest, shortness of breath, fatigue and soreness for days thereafter. In fact, my whole sternal area was tender. The targeted acupoint [i.e. acupuncture point] in the chest was Ren17 (*dan zhong* or *shan zhong*), translated as "Chest Center," "Upper Sea of Chi," or "The Source," which gives you an idea of its function – and of my problem, namely, it is a gathering point for chi and a strong tonifying point of chi in the chest. (You could think of it acting as a traffic cop in the center of a multi-road intersection.) Ren17 corresponds to the "Lower Sea of Chi" point, Ren6 (*qi hai*), located at a space of two fingers below the navel on the body's midline. "This area," say Ellis, Wiseman, and Boss in their book, *Grasping the Wind*, "serves as a reservoir of qi for the whole of the body. It is the place from which qi emanates and to which it returns, and is thus the Sea of Qi."[2] It is also known as the "dan tian."

What happened to me, I think, was that my Ren17 area was over-stimulated by the empty force striking it through the crystal – just too much chi at once, thereby jamming up the main thoroughfare of the chest, causing the shortness of breath, pain, and fatigue. Just as at rush hour, it took a long time to dissipate. Actually, the symptoms were alleviated when Ren17 was needled with a reducing-method technique.

From these experiences, I certainly gained a healthy respect for the power of empty force chi kung, and learned to appreciate the need for the chi in the body to flow naturally, without impediments.

I've taken my lessons in chi into my practice of acupuncture at the clinic. When I work with a patient, I look to see where the chi has "clumped together" (where the traffic jams have occurred), or where the chi has "run out of gas," so to speak. This provides me with important clues toward the treating of patients. With such clues, then, through applying needles and external chi, I can regulate the patient's chi flow, bringing harmony back to the highways of his or her body.

I feel that my sensitivity to chi was awakened in my student days during the chi kung classes with Paul Dong. I'm very grateful to him for having shared his knowledge, and for having opened me to the personal experience of chi, to know it not just as an academic concept, but rather as a living, dynamic, essential force of life. It's made all the difference. Thank you, Paul.

## References

1 Maciocia, G., 1989, *The Foundations of Chinese Medicine: A Comprehensive Text for Acupuncturists and Herbalists*, Churchill Livingstone, New York, p. 36.
2 Ellis, A., Wiseman, N., Boss, K., 1989, *Grasping the Wind*, Paradigm Publications, Brookline, Mass., p. 309.

Karen Cameron, c/o Paul Dong
P.O. Box 2011
Oakland, CA 94604, U.S.A.

Karen Cameron is a specialist in Chinese medicine, including acupuncture, herbal medicine and chi kung. She holds the title Diplomate Acupuncture from the U.S. National Commission for the Certification of Acupuncturists (currently recognized for licensing purposes in about 40 states of the U.S.).


EMPTY FORCE AND THE BUTTERFLY EFFECT
by James P. Coats

I first came across empty force chi kung in the book *Chi Gong: An Ancient Chinese Way to Health* by Paul Dong and Aristide H.

Esser. As the book did not describe the details of the exercise, I decided to contact Master Dong in order to find out more about the methods of practice and the background to the development of the skill. Although I have not yet been able to expend as much time on practice as I would wish, nevertheless I will endeavor to put down some observations and ideas which may be of some use.

It is generally accepted that the most essential element of the standing and sitting postures is relaxation. However, this is not always easy to accomplish in a static position. Obviously some tension is necessary, otherwise the body would collapse in an amorphous heap on the floor. What is required is to utilize the minimum tension to maintain the posture. I have found two procedures helpful in this respect. First, if movement across a joint is loose and easy, it usually indicates relaxation, although it is not the cause of relaxation. This looseness is caused by less and less tension being used by the contracting and extending muscles which effect the movement across the joint. So, by gradually reducing the motion and retaining the easy sensation, the relaxed state can be transferred to the motionless posture. This may also be the rationale behind those Taoist exercises which employ shaking of the limbs.

The second helpful procedure is to sense the minimum tension needed to maintain the posture against gravity. This entails finding that point of balance at which more tension would cause the arms or legs to rise, and less tension would cause them to sink. Once again, relaxation in the motionless posture is attained through smaller and smaller movements, until the balance point is reached. It is estimated in the main chi kung clinics in China that it usually takes about six months to master relaxation to an effective degree. In my practice I have observed some of the usual normal effects, such as shaking of the body initially, perspiration, improved digestion, and a warm sensation, sometimes localized and sometimes general.

Natural breathing is used in empty force chi kung; this is conditioned by both the relaxed posture and the mental state. Sometimes my breathing seemed to speed up; and at other times it slowed down and almost stopped.

"The Butterfly Effect" is often used as an illustration in a recent branch of mathematics which deals with apparently chaotic systems in nature. The idea is that the flight of a butterfly in an English garden on a warm summer afternoon may trigger a series of events in the atmosphere which will eventually culminate in a powerful hurricane many thousands of miles away. It has been stated that the most important requirement in chi kung is mental quietude, without which the effectiveness of the exercise is greatly diminished. It is stressed that this quietude must be *allowed* to happen, rather than *made* to happen. This can be difficult to grasp for the Western ego, which is used to exerting strength in order to accomplish a goal. The opposite of what is needed – anxiety and tension, for example – will be produced by such striving. A spiritual attitude is needed, the abolishing of desire for the fruit of your labor. So, do not expend a lot of energy and tension on chasing it around the garden – better to stand calmly or sit down quietly, and maybe, after a little while, and when you least expect it, the butterfly of tranquility will alight upon your head.

James P. Coats
"Lakeside"
Grands Vaux
St. Saviour
Jersey, JEZ 7NA, England

James P. Coats is a musician and chi kung practitioner.


## OBSERVATIONS ON THE EMPTY FORCE AND CHI KUNG
by William Chun

The ancient yet novel concept of the empty force attracted me into the world of chi kung. As I remember it, I watched Master Paul Dong make students move without physical contact in the summer of 1982 at the San Francisco YMCA. I was skeptical at the time, but I joined his chi kung class out of curiosity.

Six months later, I came to know Master Cai Songfang from Guangzhou, China, who used the empty force to push a six-foot-tall Caucasian student ten yards back. The student could offer no resistance. At the same time, I also met a master, M. Ng, living in San Francisco, who taught me how to create chi and emit it. I often practiced with these three masters, and finally I began to start experiencing something of the mysteries of the empty force.

There are great differences in the external chi, or empty force energy, sent out by different masters. Now, I would like to describe my personal impressions of them.

Master Cai's empty force energy is fine like a thread, cannot be pinned down, and, if resisted, causes disturbances and over-stimulation in the chi and blood circulation. Once, a group of eight of us were standing around him in a circle and practicing the standing-on-stake of wuji (boundless) style chi kung. He was just standing motionless in the center, but all of us felt a stream of warm chi rising from the feet and making the whole body warm. This warmth lasted two or three minutes. However, even after that, a Mr. Gan, who was standing next to me, remained unsteady on his feet, his forehead sweating. Later, Mr. Gan told us that he felt as though someone were pushing his foot and he couldn't stand steady, no matter how much he exerted self-control. Mr. Gan is a master of Wu style tai chi and should never be unsteady on his feet, but faced with the empty force he could offer no resistance.

Master Ng sends the empty force from his hands, but he has no set hand motions. He has two kinds of energy, gentle and tough. The former brings a feeling of warm numbness, and the latter feels boiling hot and makes a person lose balance. On one unforgettable Saturday, a few students were sitting and chatting, and I was sitting in meditation in a chair about six feet away, when, suddenly, Master Ng shouted at me to look at his forehead. I looked up, opening my eyes wide, and at that moment I felt myself being raised from my chair by a mysterious power coming from his forehead. I asked him if he used the empty force from his third eye, but he just smiled.

Master Dong's empty force feels like gusts of wind. It can make a group of students lose balance. He usually uses one hand or both hands to send it. He has the students stand in a line and sends his energy to them. It has very strong penetrating power and can go through more than ten people, a thick wooden board or a brick wall.

I might also mention another of my chi kung instructors, Xi Changfang. His empty force feels like pressure. If one doesn't dissipate the chi, it will overstimulate the chi and blood circulation, make the face hot and cause dizziness.

These are my impressions of the empty force. (No doubt others have their own experiences or impressions.) There is an ancient

Chinese legend concerning the "mystery palm," which might be the same as the modern-day empty force. We can't explain this mysterious force with modern mechanics, and it is difficult to measure with present-day scientific instruments. It could be related to the electrical fields of the human body. This force can not only knock a person down but can also cause injury if used improperly, and induce feelings of cold, warmth, and numbness. Its mysteries remain to be explained by future scientific research.

William Chun
American Chinese Qi Gong Study Association
619 Kearny St.
San Francisco, CA 94108, U.S.A.

William Chun, the first chairperson and president of the American Chinese Qi Gong Study Association, is an engineer for NASA (the American space exploration agency).

## IN-BETWEEN EXPERIENCE OF EMPTY FORCE
by Jane Hallander

Empty force, or ling kong jing in Chinese, is one of the great mysteries of chi kung practice. Some say it's the ultimate martial art technique. Others claim it doesn't exist, except as a figment of a chi kung practitioner's mind.

My own experience is somewhere in-between. My chi kung teachers, Pengxi You and, later, his wife Min Ou Yang, both used ling kong jing. It was not specifically taught to their students, but was a natural by-product of their chi kung practice. It was never emphasized as a martial technique, because its dramatic effects are seen only in chi kung practitioners who have developed the ability to keep substantial amounts of chi close to their bodies, using it as a buffer against the ling kong jing. In other words, if someone who did not practice chi kung rushed you while out on the street, your ling kong jing energy would pass through his body – at best making him ill several days later. It would do nothing to help you in the immediate self-defense situation.

As I learned it, empty force was a tool to gauge your own, and others', chi development. For those emitting ling kong jing, their partner's reaction was a test of how strong their own chi power was. Conversely, those responding to ling kong jing emission are able to gauge their own sensitivity to, and ability to combat, another person's chi.

The ability to use ling kong jing comes from developing strong, smooth-flowing chi channels. Where the average person's chi is easily dispersed and scattered from the body, chi kung practitioners who have done a lot of standing meditation (*zhan zhuang*) have chi that adheres to their bodies as if in a thick, closely-packed formation.

Chi is emitted from their bodies through a process the Chinese call *shen, yi, chi*. Shen is spirit, yi is intention and chi is the internal energy or force. When these three come together and are directed at a target through the chi kung practitioner's eyes, the result, providing their chi is strong enough, can be ling kong jing.

Using yi (intention), a ling kong jing practitioner can cause the other person to do many different gymnastic movements – from leaping in the air to somersaults or rolls. I have seen and experienced all of these, including being forced to the ground where I could not move until my teacher released me.

The feeling from ling kong jing is difficult to explain. The person emitting empty force often feels a subtle connection between the fingertips and the general area around the recipient, who sometimes feels as if he or she had run into a brick wall. One outcome, however, is universal for those receiving ling kong jing: if their chi is weaker than that of the person transmitting, they will have no physical strength or mental desire to counter his or her will.

Ling kong jing is developed through daily standing meditation ("standing-on-stake") and special chi kung exercise practice. Standing meditation develops chi that is stronger and more quickly rejuvenated. Exercises that teach the chi kung stylist to emit chi from his or her fingers develop the ability to send chi out of the whole body.

Some chi kung doctors in China use ling kong jing for healing purposes, sending chi into patients' bodies to affect pressure points (acupuncture points) in the areas they wish to treat. Their training is the same. My original teacher, Professor Pengxi You, trained many of the doctors at Shanghai's chi kung hospital.

He once used ling kong jing on me to relieve the symptoms of advanced heat stroke. I was almost at the point of passing out, with cold clammy skin and a very pale complexion. He used a ling kong jing technique called "fanning" to enable his stronger chi to open my blocked energy channels. Within five minutes, I had regained my strength. My skin was normal in temperature and appearance, and I suffered no energy loss – a rate of recovery that is almost unheard of in Western medicine.

Jane Hallander
5603C Paradise Dr.
Corte Madera, CA 94925, U.S.A.

Ms Hallander is a martial arts master and writer.


## AN EMPTY FORCE SKEPTIC
by Elliot Harvey

Let me begin this article by admitting that I *was* a skeptic. I was one of those people who kept buying videos and books, and taking classes from so-called masters, in the hope of learning the amazing healing techniques they promised. I was invariably disappointed; and so I became increasingly skeptical. I have witnessed such phenomena as bringing dead flies back to life, breaking enormous amounts of bricks, having a truck roll across a person's stomach, and more. I'm not saying that there aren't true masters who can perform these acts (I've met only one) but most such acts have been tricks.

A short time ago, I read an article about a man who claimed that he could do chi projection (empty force). One of my goals has always been to defeat an opponent with empty force. Since obtaining my Master credential in acupressure and becoming a Black Sash in Chinese Kung-Fu, I have been wanting to learn it all the more.

I travelled to Oakland to meet Master Paul Dong. My skepticism travelled along with me. Would this be a person who could actually perform, or was he only another trickster?

When Master Dong asked me to do certain exercises to see if I was susceptible to chi energy, I did all I could do to fight against feeling anything. If this was going to be true chi projection, I didn't want to let it have any advantages. I closed my eyes; I blanked my mind; I tensed up – all to no avail. I felt The Energy. My hands started to vibrate, I felt stinging and tingling together. IT WAS REAL . . .

The empty force that Master Dong was generating started to affect my insides. I felt very disoriented as well as nauseous and dizzy. It was working!

As we all know, this ability to project empty force is not something one can achieve overnight. But, with daily practice and the guidance of Master Paul Dong, one should eventually be able to master it. I feel very fortunate to have taken private sessions with Master Dong.

In conclusion, I have found Master Dong to be honorable and truthful, as well as a true empty force master.

Elliot Harvey
3363 Tuxford Pl.
Thousand Oaks, CA 91360, U.S.A.

Mr. Harvey has been in martial arts for many years.


## TRUE ENERGY: CHI KUNG
by Ying Zhong Lu (Ying Jong Leu)

Chi Kung is an arcane discipline of the Orient, as well as a very effective health method. Thousands of years of tradition, plus modern research combining medicine, physics, and biology have given us quite a good scientific understanding of chi kung.

Not only is chi kung widespread in Mainland China, it is quite popular in Taiwan too. There are many chi kung practice groups of different traditions, and frequent chi kung lectures which draw audiences of thousands. The reason is that everyone wants to improve his or her health through chi kung.

I am not a professional chi kung scholar, but I have practiced *jian yi chi kung* ("simple" chi kung), *xiang gong* ("fragrance practice"), and other styles. I experienced a sense of physical comfort in the bones and muscles, and I came to realize that chi kung is indeed a true form of energy. Particularly in the last 20 years, I have followed UFO and ESP research, and I am deeply convinced that there are many kinds of force and truth beyond our current human understanding.

Based on my experience, the body can put out a "chi flow," a kind of "energy flow" that can be moved through the body at will to strengthen the body's resistance to illness. Indeed, it can "massage" the internal organs to strengthen all kinds of internal body functions. In addition, these personal energy flows can interact with a universal energy flow, clearing the internal body, purifying the spirit body, and achieving the stage of *tian ren he yi* ("the unity of Heaven and man"), which brings an understanding of many cosmic principles.

I believe there is much that can be learned by entering the "chi kung state." That is, we can receive information from higher intelligences in the universe.

As humankind marches on toward the 21st century, chi kung can come into its own to the benefit of humanity. We must preserve such a meaningful force.

Paul Dong and I are old friends. We are both researchers in chi kung, psychics, and UFOs. With this little essay I hope to celebrate the publication of his new book and express some ideas about chi kung.

Ying Zhong Lu (Ying Jong Leu)
Professor, Fo Kuang University
Chairman, Taiwan UFO Society
P.O. Box 36-270
Taipei 105, Taiwan

Ying Zhong Lu is a professor in Taiwan who does psychic, UFO, and chi kung research.


## EMPTY FORCE: A POSITIVE ADDICTION
by Steven Michael Matias

My first real introduction to chi kung was a dramatic and unforgettable one. In the spring of 1991, my fiancée took me to an open house night at the San Francisco College of Acupuncture, where she was then a student. It was also where Paul Dong was teaching his standing-on-stake and energy healing styles of chi kung. The previous year we had read his book on this ancient Chinese art, one of the five branches of traditional Oriental medicine, along with acupuncture, herbology, massage, and nutrition. I was intrigued by what I had heard about the demonstrations of external chi power that he was doing at the college.

Upon our meeting, he had me hold out a hand while he projected some chi into my palm to see if I was "sensitive" to the energy. A cool invisible wave seemed to pass through my hand

and a sensation of numbness began spreading into my fingers and wrist. When I told him this, he declared: "I can knock you on your back with my chi." Oh, you can't do anything of the kind, I thought; but I made a non-committal reply and agreed to let him try. He stood about 12–15 feet away from me and I closed my eyes so as not to be influenced by anything he was doing.

After a few seconds, I found myself swaying back and forth on the spot, and then suddenly falling backward and crashing into some chairs. I picked myself up with the laughter of the other students ringing in my ears. They had all had similar experiences themselves at the hands of Master Dong. It was as if a cloud, or a gas – invisible and odorless – had come over me. The sensation was not like a lightning bolt but rather like being hit with a puff of air or a feather, or nothing at all – emptiness itself. My mind raced to find an explanation. Did I lose my balance because my eyes were closed? No; I felt firmly in control at the time. Was it just suggestion? No hypnotic induction had been done. Could the force of the mysterious chi have caused it? Needless to say, this piqued my interest in learning the method and I began practicing the zhan zhuang or standing-on-stake form for most of the rest of the year.

In early February of 1992, Master Dong began instructing me in ling kong jing, the "empty force" chi kung he had used on me in the demonstration. He explained it would produce the strongest amount of chi energy but would take longer to learn than other styles. I started with one half-hour standing and sitting meditation daily, quickly moved up to over an hour after two months and after three never did less than 90 minutes. The practice was simplicity itself: a few seemingly easy moving, standing and seated postures. The challenge was to hold them for increasing lengths of time, while doing certain inner visualizations and at other times emptying the mind of all thought. I deliberately refrained from studying the theory of Oriental medicine so as not to prejudice the experience.

From the first day, I could feel the sensation of chi – like a gentle electric current running through various parts of my body, sometimes even into specific fingers and toes. This was very different from the fizzy, bubbling feelings of chi that I had while practicing the standing-on-stake style. It became easier to make distinctions between the various subtle and gross sensations I was experiencing, from heavy pins-and-needles prickling, to hot flashes wrapping around my legs; from tingling and distention in the extremities, to movements of silk-thread-like fineness. I was beginning to feel as if I were an electric eel.

Five months into the practice, the "small circuit" opened: I woke up one morning with the energy current doing a loop down the front of the torso, up the back and over the head with lightning-like rapidity. I lay there for a while, enjoying the feeling. My tongue had automatically stretched up to the roof of my mouth to connect the circuit. And it has remained there ever since – except when I talk or consciously bring it down. Soon afterwards, I could sense the chi radiating out from the belly and moving simultaneously through the arms and legs as the "large circuit" developed. The sensations grew progressively stronger during the first year, especially in the hands, feet and dan tian, as I learned to extend the chi into the earth and sky and other people.

There were many periods when I remained on long plateaux in the practice – neither progressing nor falling back in chi development. But I learned that it was important to stay with the discipline. People who do the exercise consistently make progress, and those who don't, don't.

The sitting meditation became gradually deeper as well. Where once thoughts crowded in, and my thought process ran on of its own accord; later, the mind would fall instantly silent as soon as I sat down. More and more, I would enter a state of consciousness that can only be described inadequately as a quivering silence or an energetic void. Often a deep peace would settle in my body. At certain times my normal sense of self seemed to disappear and I became an expanding, ecstatic field of chi.

I had first become interested in yoga and meditation in 1964. After many years of sitting, it was a relief to get up out of the cross-legged postures and stand. Since the chi kung meditations are done sitting upright on a chair with feet flat on the ground, it was possible to sit far longer than I ever could in the full lotus position. And it permitted a freer flow of energy throughout the legs. The build-up of chi is especially strong if one sits more than 30 minutes.

There were physical results, too. My stamina and vitality increased, the muscles in the arms and legs and back got stronger, and my capacity for self-healing awakened. Once, doing some heavy lifting at work, I strained the muscles in my right arm so badly that I could not turn the pages of a book without pain. After I did my chi kung the next morning, all the discomfort vanished and did not return. On one occasion, when my gums were swollen and painful, I applied my hands to them and visualized the chi flowing to the affected areas, which reduced the pain considerably, almost to nothing. Some white pigment spots that I've had on my arms for years have returned to normal color, perhaps due to increased circulation of blood and chi. I have found from experience that even a little chi kung can squeeze aches and pains and fatigue right out of the body.

For a time, the chi seemed to be stuck in the area of my chest, just buzzing around in the center of the heart, even after practice was concluded. I asked Master Dong if I should try to move it down to the dan tian. "The chi knows what to do," he advised. "Just let it go where it will." It does indeed seem to have an intelligence of its own which works to correct the imbalances of the practitioner in a safe manner. The only injuries that have ever occurred to me were a slight soreness in the right knee and a mild muscle strain in the left shoulder. Both happened in the early days of practice and quickly went away.

With the chi channels open and functioning, the next stage was to extend the chi out of my body into others. This aspect of empty force has a martial arts application, though this is a subject of much controversy. My interest, however, is in health, in spiritual practice, and in investigating the subtle energy body of the meridians and acupoints.

Now over two years into the method, practicing a couple of hours or more at a stretch is easy and comfortable. It has become a "positive addiction" to which I've happily succumbed. This discipline has given me a quiet mind and calm emotions, and has made me a more balanced person. My hope is to work someday as a chi kung therapist with my fiancée who is training to be an acupuncturist and herbalist. I can't imagine a life without chi kung.

Steven Matias, c/o Paul Dong
P.O. Box 2011
Oakland, CA 94604, U.S.A.

Steven Matias is a reiki healer and empty force practitioner.

## EXPERIENCES IN PRACTICE OF LING KONG JING
by Richard M. Mooney

My name is Richard M. Mooney, and I am a 34-year-old martial arts practitioner. I've been active in Asian martial arts since the age of 10. My original ability to project empty force came about as a natural outgrowth of my training in the tai chi ruler system of chi kung, but the rate of energy development was very slow, and only after 3 to 4 years of dedicated practice was I able to issue jing, as well as to heal with chi on a limited basis. My discovery that I had this ability came about quite accidentally. One evening during class, I was demonstrating technical aspects of a type of punch. As I slowly moved my fist forward, the student in front of me lost his balance. I thought this was very curious, and so I performed the same action again: the same result occurred. I then asked the rest of the class, one by one, to stand before me. I was able to achieve the same results with varying degrees of success.

This incident got me to thinking about some of the so-called legendary powers of martial arts masters of the past, with their power to throw people far away with hardly a touch, or to cause severe damage with just a touch. I had also read that such skill only came about after long training in chi kung – some accounts stated that at least 10 years was required. Such a period of time did not, I thought, seem unreasonable, given my progress to date through the practice of tai chi ruler. With that in mind, I continued my training in the ruler system.

Then, one day, fate stepped in. I was browsing in a book store when I came upon a book that was written by Master Paul Dong and Dr. Aristide Esser. The title of the book was *Chi Gong: An Ancient Chinese Way to Health*. A chapter on the empty force enabled me to begin to understand a little more about the ability I was gaining. I was determined to find the address of Master Dong. Fate stepped in again – in the form of a magazine called *Qigong*, to which I had a subscription. Lo and behold, there was Master Dong on the cover! I read his article and, at the end, found his address. That was in February of 1993. When I wrote to Master Dong, asking him if he could teach me his method, his reply came back very quickly, along with his phone number. After having a very pleasant talk we came to an agreement, and, having sent him a small fee for his information, I began my practice of ling kong jing: the empty force.

At first glance the practice of "standing still" seems to be quite boring, but let me be the first to tell you that it is anything but dull! The training is very arduous, and requires a great deal of willpower, determination, and focus. In the first few weeks of my practice I thought my arms and legs were going to fall off! Sweat poured off me in rivers, and many thoughts would just pop into my mind without any apparent reason. Then, as the weeks passed, the pains in the arms and legs would diminish, as would the profuse sweating and rambling thoughts. I started to sense certain things that were going on inside me: a subtle tingling was making itself felt all over my body, and a noticeable warmth was wrapping itself about my lower legs, from my knees to my ankles. This warmth would last for many, many hours, and might best be compared to having Tiger Balm rubbed all over the lower legs. This happened about eight weeks into my practice, and, after a few weeks longer, never happened again.

Other things then began to occur in about week 16 of my training. I began to feel certain acupoints opening up and expanding. The feelings were quite pleasant, and along with this came other sensations: a strong current of electric heat in my hands, for instance; a feeling that my body was transparent and empty; and also a feeling that at times I would enter a state of complete emptiness. I did not notice if I was breathing, or if I had been "standing" long. It was as if time had ceased to exist, or that I were existing outside of time. That state of mind is something that I will always enjoy being in!

Now, as for the physical development I gained from standing, my thighs went from being big and round to being bigger and very well defined. My back and my shoulders also saw an increase in muscle build-up, and the standing started to become less of a chore and more of an enjoyment. My breathing also underwent a drastic change.

During my tai chi practice, my breathing was about five breaths per minute. Now that I had been "standing" about four months, my breaths slowed to about three breaths per minute while "standing," and as low as two breaths per minute during the silent sitting meditation period that always follows the standing practice. My total practice was about two-and-a-half hours per day at this point.

Of course, during this time I was also testing my ability to project chi and knock people off balance. My ability to do this was increasing, not only in terms of force, but also in terms of flexibility – what I could do with it. I also discovered that not everyone is equally affected by the empty force. Some would go staggering back when I projected at them; others would be gently taken off balance; still others were totally unaffected. I attributed this to one of two reasons: either my force was not yet strong enough, or they had some kind of immunity to what I was emitting. (I guess this can be compared to someone who can go out on the town and consume a lot of drinks without getting a hangover while someone else who only has a few drinks feels miserable all next day.) My first hypothesis was proved by a person whom I was unable to move one day, yet 30 days later was made to move back when I projected chi.

Now, as to depth of my ability, I can only say that it is not confined to being able to make someone step back. It can also be used, in my case, to ward off punches and kicks as well as grabs to any part of my body – wrists, chest, throat, legs, shoulders, and neck. Those who are sensitive to the energy say that it feels as if their hands are very heavy and they cannot hang on. Still others have said that their hands feel very hot so that, if they hang on any longer, they will burn them. I have also found that if someone who is sensitive tries to strike or kick me, I can throw him or her to the ground by projecting energy into the attacking limb. In addition, I can project this energy into anything I happen to be holding, be it a club or a nightstick, a staff or a sword. If he or she tries to grab the weapon, it is the same as if he or she were trying to grab me – and is forced off. I have also tried another experiment in which I ask one student to grab another. Then I project my energy into the second student and the attacker is compelled to let go, just as if he or she were grabbing me.

Finally, I have been able to project the energy through walls of concrete and doors made of wood, with varying degrees of success. At this point I can attribute any weakness in my empty force to the fact that I have now been training for only 15 months. I wonder what I will be capable of in 15 years . . .

This brings me to my next point – how is this ability made manifest within the human body? Either I can subscribe to the Eastern concepts of chi, jing, and shen (spirit) by which energy is accumulated in the lower dan tian and made to circulate through the small and then large "circuits" of the body – before being projected outside with sufficient power to affect others; or, I can look at it in Western terms, something I can understand with less confusion. In the Western view, I might speculate that the body is put under a specific type of stress, which causes the brain to secrete certain chemical compounds. I believe that these work in one of two ways: either they open an unused area of the brain that allows us to project the empty force, or they saturate the body to such a degree that they themselves cause the empty force effect. It is my hope that one day a thorough study of this ability will be made, and the answer found within my lifetime.

That brings me to my last point – how the public views this ability, and its standing in the martial arts community at large. As a martial artist I have the honor of putting on demonstrations at a variety of functions for various civic groups and schools. As part of my presentation I always touch on the limitless power of the mind, and to that end I always use the ability I have gained through my ling kong jing practice. There are those who accept my demonstration with an open mind; those who feel that this part of the demonstration is "fixed," and think they are being deceived; and those of a superstitious temperament who resort to the use of the words "magic" or "witchcraft."

I respect each person's opinion, for that is how he or she is; but to those who discount this ability, I have a challenge: if you would dismiss it as fraud or magic, train in it yourself to get to the truth of the matter.

Richard M. Mooney
Sarasota Shao-Lin Academy
4655 Flatbush Ave.
Sarasota, FL 34233, U.S.A.

Richard Mooney is a martial arts instructor teaching kung-fu and tai chi ruler. He has studied the empty force under Paul Dong.

## LEARNING EMPTY FORCE FOR SELF-HEALING
by Rosa Mui

I am vice-president of an engineering company. I was introduced to chi kung by my husband, Paul Mui. In the beginning, he and I had no experience and did not really believe in chi kung. My husband started when he was on disability leave, due to stress. Because Western medicine did not help him, he tried to learn chi kung to relax himself and to lower his stress level.

One day, I hurt my left arm and could not move it. The doctors did not know what the trouble was. Other than giving me medication for pain, they could not help me. So my husband used his chi kung healing power to try to fix my arm. I could feel the warm wave of energy bathing my muscles. Within minutes, I could move my arm slowly. He then taught me how to generate chi myself to heal my arm. Within twenty-four hours, it had returned to normal. After that experience, I became very interested in chi kung and asked him to teach me more. Since then, I have been practicing whenever I have the time.

I was eager to learn more and, eventually, had an opportunity to meet with Master Paul Dong who taught me the higher level chi kung called empty force. About a year ago, Master Dong was giving a healing, using his mind and his hands to pass his chi to me. I could feel his healing power run throughout my body, instantly increasing my energy level. Because of my experience with Master Dong, I now practice the empty force every day, not for martial arts, but for better health and self-healing.

Rosa Mui
4116 Folsom Dr.
Antioch, CA 94509, U.S.A.

Rosa Mui is a chi kung practitioner and vice-president of an engineering company.

## STUDENT CLAIMS TO BEND CANDLE FLAME
by Jerry Pool

It's been an honor to have Paul Dong as my teacher. I've always had a strong desire in my heart to achieve skills that are not easily gained. Since I began my training in empty force, I've gained more serenity and become much more understanding as a person. I've never felt better or healthier than I feel now. When I was a younger man, my heart was full of rage and anger. Now I feel at peace for the first time in my life. I owe this change to my training in the empty force.

I practice daily for two to three hours. Sometimes I reach such deep levels of relaxation that I feel as if my body had become transparent. When I focus on my hands they become "full," as if congested, and sometimes it seems that they will explode. Other people tell me they can feel my energy on their bodies as small electric shocks. I've recently started projecting on to a candle. I simply sit in a chair and project my thoughts at the flame and it will bend in any direction I want. I can do this at a distance of six to eight feet from the candle. I've now been practicing for one and a half years. Everything I have gained has been very positive. To everyone who is interested in this type of training, I would say "please give it an honest try." Your effort will be well rewarded. Best wishes to all of you in your training. I feel certain you will never give it up. I know I never will.

Jerry Pool
2024 JR Deputy
Little Rock, Arkansas 72205, U.S.A.

Jerry Pool is a martial arts, empty force and chi kung practitioner.

# Afterword

## EMPTY FORCE AND EXCEPTIONAL HUMAN FUNCTIONING

The style of chi kung called ling kong jing, or "empty force," has several applications. Among these are health promotion, fitness, increased longevity, and the emission of chi for healing or for martial arts purposes. In this afterword, we shall examine its role in developing the abilities known as "exceptional human functioning" and its potential as a form of meditation or spiritual practice. Exceptional human functions, as the Chinese call them (hereafter abbreviated as EHF), are equivalent to the siddhis of the Hindu and Buddhist yogic traditions and the psi phenomena, or psychic powers, of the Western world. We believe that chi kung generally, and the specific set of standing, moving, and sitting postures that generate the empty force, can be considered as a form of yoga or a system of psycho-physical development which can lead to various transformations of the human mind/body/ spirit continuum.

Though chi kung has a history stretching back more than three millennia, it is only in the last fifteen years that the little-known and esoteric form of it – ling kong jing – has begun to be taught in the West. It has been attracting increasing attention among martial artists and health care practitioners, both in Mainland China and in the United States, because of its particular relevance to those disciplines. But our focus here will be on its potential for engendering an extraordinary life of the mind and spirit.

The major study of exceptional human functioning in our time is *The Future of the Body: Explorations into the Further Evolution of Human Nature*, written by the philosopher/psychologist Michael Murphy. This work places EHF in a wide evolutionary framework. It is Murphy's thesis that all twelve of the basic

119

human abilities and attributes (outlined below) can in certain circumstances give way to higher, "metanormal" versions of themselves. And he places them in the context of an evolutionary leap that the human race can, but not necessarily will, make.

Just as the universe evolved living beings out of inorganic matter, so did it transcend itself a second time with the appearance of mankind and the subsequent psycho-social evolution of human cultures. Murphy believes that a third kind of evolutionary transcendence may be in the offing as human beings learn to develop their normal abilities and to alter their bodies and environment into metanormal levels. He defines metanormal events and processes as those that are radically new, unexplainable on current scientific principles, and mediated by agencies such as the Divine, the Buddha-nature, the Tao, grace, chi, Spirit, etc. Also assisting in the movement from the normal to the super-normal are what he calls transformative and integral practices. The former he defines as "a complex and coherent set of activities that produce positive changes in a person or group." These could include religion, athletics, the arts, psychotherapy, and even marriage and child-rearing. Integral practices, on the other hand, are those that "cultivate the physical, vital, affective, cognitive, volitional, and transpersonal dimensions of human functioning in an integrated way." Examples might include Patanjali's eight-limbed yoga, psychosynthesis, Zen Buddhism, the purna yoga of Sri Aurobindo, and aikido. However, in his view, complete integral practices that develop all these attributes concurrently are yet to be created.

The accompanying chart, adapted from *The Future of the Body*, outlines Murphy's "twelve-step program" for future human evolution. These twelve attributes are not meant to be exhaustive; others could be added. Nor are they water-tight compartments, for they can interfuse and overlap. They are further subdivided into three categories: first, the products of ordinary mammalian evolution; second, the normal abilities developed by human acculturation; and third, examples of extraordinary functioning.

How does all this apply to the art and science of chi kung? Empty force and the other forms of chi kung, as well as the martial arts and sports generally, can be put into a larger context than has previously been envisioned. Examples can be given of many, if not most, of the attributes being produced through the practice of empty force – particularly vitality, perception, pain

| The attributes | Ordinary Mammalian Evolution | Normal Human Aculturations | Extraordinary Functions |
|---|---|---|---|
| I. Perception of External Events | Animal and human perception mediated by eyes, ears, nose, and skin | Trained sensory awareness in sports, psychology, meditation | Extrasensory perception and extended sensory functioning |
| II. Psycholphysical Awareness and Self-Regulation | Brain and nervous systems | Kinesthetic sense in athletics and the creative arts | Metanormal internal perception and bodily control |
| III. Communication | Normal visual or auditory or aural signalling | Developed verbal and nonverbal transmissions | Telepathy, spiritual healing, shared mystical experience |
| IV. Vitality | Warm-bloodedness, chemical and electric energy | Strength and fitness training, increased stamina | Extraordinary energies of qi, prana, kundalini |
| V. Movement | Bodily structures of arms, legs, wings, fins | Ordinary agility | Levitation, out-of-body travel, shamanic journeys |
| VI. Environmental Alteration | Mammalian hands, feet, mouths | | Telekinesis, distant healing, qi power |
| VII. Pleasure and Pain | Sensations of nervous systems | Specialized disciplines of education, sports, technology | Extraordinary bliss and joy of religious experience |
| VIII. Cognition | Sense organs, brain and nervous systems | Sensory awareness training, sports, therapy | Pre and retro cognition, yogic knowledge by identity |
| IX. Volition | Ordinary goal-directed action, intention | Developmental training in education, arts, sciences | Surrender to the Divine or Tao, Wu Wei (purposeless purpose) |
| X. Individuation and Sense of Self | Unique individuality in higher life forms | Strengthened willpower via religion, martial arts, psychology | Ego transcending union with the Divine and all life |
| XI. Love | Mammalian mating, care for young, self-sacrificial behavior | Healthy ego identity through education, therapy | Bliss of Divine union, ananda of meditation |
| XII. Bodily Structures and Processes | Organs, circulatory systems | Human affection, compassion, empathy | Meridians, chakras, nadis, higher bodies, subtle matter, morphogenic fields |
| | | Somatic training, muscular and skeletal articulation | |

into pleasure, individuality, volition, communication, and alteration both of the environment and of bodily structures. In his book *Chi Gong: An Ancient Chinese Way to Health*, Paul Dong gives several anecdotal accounts of the extraordinary powers of ling kong jing masters.

One of the most dramatic effects reported by empty force practitioners is their ability to move or injure other people at a distance. Whether this is due to the action of chi power, or to a sophisticated kind of intentional role-playing, is hotly disputed among martial artists – as is its efficacy as a form of self-defense. However, scientific support for the empty force has been provided by Dr. Liu Guo Long of the Beijing College of Traditional Chinese Medicine. He monitored the brain functioning of human subjects and animals, and found that chi kung masters could affect a measurable change in the EEG patterns of both, without contact or any normal means of communication. The fact that animals were equally influenced would seem to rule out a placebo effect or suggestion. Thus we can see how several of the metanormal analogues of the attributes can be manifested in one event – in this case, volition, communication, vitality, and alteration of the environment.

The practice of chi kung, especially the more powerful forms such as ling kong jing, can produce both extraordinary energy and vitality, and supernormal bodily structures such as the chi channels or meridians. (This is the case whether one regards the meridians as pre-existing or as "formed" through the practice itself.) The opening of the major channels or "orbits," causing the sensation of heat or an electric current running through the body, is one of the foundational experiences of chi kung.

Attempts have also been made to induce EHF by projecting chi into selected acupoints on the body, particularly the points called *qi hai*, *yin tang*, and *bai hui*, all of which correspond to major chakras in the Hindu yogic system of subtle or esoteric "anatomy." These experiments are mostly carried out privately, and with varying degrees of success. We know of no controlled scientific tests which might determine their validity, but it would be intriguing to see how they performed. Indeed, it would be of great interest to do a survey of hundreds of empty force practitioners to ascertain how many of the twelve metanormal attributes not previously present could be developed over time.

We turn now to the meditative side of chi kung, which is, ultimately, its most important aspect. A variety of contemplative techniques are employed to allow the mind to become silent and still. The sitting meditation gradually reaches deeper levels over the months and years of practice. There is an increasing calm and a cessation of the thought processes, first of all for a few seconds, and then for minutes and then much longer. The few thoughts and sensations that still occur do not disturb the essential nature of the meditation. And this can lead to metanormal cognitions, a radically changed sense of identity and individuality, and a variety of altered states of consciousness very like those described in the religious and shamanic literature. These extraordinary states of awareness cannot be forced or produced on demand, but the long periods of standing and sitting, while simultaneously emptying the mind, help them to happen. As the normal, rational, waking state falls silent, it is replaced by other, metanormal processes, facilitated by increased chi flowing through open meridians.

The journalist and accomplished martial artist, Jane Hallander, has been a student of the late Dr. Pengxi You (1902–83) and his wife, Min Ou Yang, in San Francisco for over a decade (see p. 105). The Yous were among the very first to teach empty force in the West. Ms. Hallander has noted a number of transformations of body and mind during this practice over the years. Some were relatively minor, such as grey hair turning dark again, or wrinkles disappearing; others involved profound alterations of consciousness, such as out-of-body travel and classic near-death experiences, with the associated phenomena of luminosity and traveling through a tunnel. She even had one instance of apparent bilocation! While meditating in a room at her teachers' house, she was seen – simultaneously – outside in the garden by Mrs. You, who expressed surprise when she came indoors to see her student sitting there.

Ms. Hallander has also described the ability of Mrs. You to apply her external chi to push open the minute chi channels (which run from the bones to the surface of the skin) of her advanced students. This leads to increased flow of vital energy, and even at times to the apparent cessation of breathing. Of course, this has not been scientifically verified, but it is intriguing to speculate about how this could result in a reduced need for oxygen, or the ability to use it more efficiently – or perhaps even to a new way of breathing, beyond what we already do through the pores in the skin. Chi kung teacher Ken Cohen has half-jokingly referred to oxygen as "a poison," since it is instrumental in the formation of free radicals in the cells, which are involved in the ageing process.

Yet another by-product of the empty force is a strongly developed intentional consciousness and the ability to be aware of the intentions of others at a subtle level. Fong Ha of Berkeley, California, who has practiced empty force and the related art of "boundless" force since the early 1980s, has compared this to the ability of blind people and animals to sense when someone is staring at them. Sifu Ha has described his experience while engaged in tai chi "push hands" practice with his colleague Cai Songfang and his students. So sensitive were they to his intention as soon as it had formed, that they could neutralize his every move. In Sifu Ha's understanding, ling kong jing is not an irresistible power that bowls people over, but an almost physical awareness of, and response to, chi fields. And this *ting jing*, or subtle perception of energy and intent, has applications in the martial arts and other areas as well.

Though commonly considered a method for improving health, extending life-span, and generating increased chi for martial arts uses, ling kong jing, like other forms of meditation, does partly address the spiritual dimension. Empty force should probably be categorized as a transformative, and not an integral, practice since it is not primarily oriented to the spiritual levels of human attainment. But even though its main focus is on health and self-defense, every psycho-physical discipline has within it the power to transcend itself and open to greater spiritual realities, even if this was not originally sought.

There are other forms of religious and alchemical chi kung which are more appropriate as candidates for full integral practice. In particular, there is the Inner Elixir School, whose earliest written records date back to the second century text of Wei Boyang, the *Zhou Yi Can Tong Ji*; but also the *yi jin jing* (muscle tendon changing) and *shii soei ching* (brain and bone marrow cleansing) – styles of chi kung invented by the Buddhist teacher Bodhidharma, or Da Mo (*c.*525). Though too complex to do anything but summarize here, they involved opening the energy gates and chi channels of the body and directing the chi deep into the bones. Common to other forms of chi kung, the small and the large microcosmic orbits, or meridian systems, had to be activated first. Next, the practice required raising the "three treasures" – jing (essence and sexual fluids), chi (internal energy), and shen (spirit consciousness) – into the upper dan tian or shen valley in the head.

In the beginning, the jing, or essence, is refined into chi in the lower dan tian for 100 days, which leads to the formation of a spiritual seed or embryo. This spiritual fetus then undergoes 10 months of "gestation" as the refined chi is converted into shen, and the spirit body grows to maturity. Then it is led by the mind, up the spine into the upper dan tian in the brain, where it undergoes three years of "nursing." Here it begins to operate independently of the body and function on subtler levels of energy and perception. The energy gate at the top of the head opens to commune with the spiritual dimension, a "return to emptiness." Finally, after nine years of "facing the wall" as Bodhidharma did, the now immortal spirit can separate from the physical body, generate other transformation bodies, and return to its original nature at the moment of bodily death (or even before) – a state known as "crushing the nothingness." In some interpretations, the physical body does not die, but becomes increasingly less material over many decades of practice until it is transformed into a supraphysical body of light. Thus the ancient dream of immortality is attained.

But whether any human has ever achieved such an apotheosis is doubtful. It is not even clear how it is to be understood. Is it a symbol for a psychological or psychic process that one can undergo? Or is it a real ontological process that can be realized? Though the alchemical chi kung comes closest to a full integral spiritual discipline, with its theory and praxis of a higher immortal body and a re-identification with the Tao/Divine, it still falls short in certain ways. It seems to lack a connection to nature, to the earth, and it could lead to a self-centered cultivation of enlightenment at the expense of human relationships and work in the world. Our interest is in a more complete spiritual practice, not another otherworldly religion.

It should be emphasized that EHF is not cultivated for its own sake, and that the supernormal is not the supernatural. The extraordinary phenomenology we have been discussing lies well within an expanded range of present human capacity and achievement. The exceptional human functions that are generated by empty force and other styles of chi kung apply by extension to many other disciplines and activities as well. Perhaps a more complete form of chi kung will be created in the future that will better harness the mysterious and miraculous power that is chi. For by these means humanity can grow into that transcendent love and grace and unitive awareness that is the heart of the spiritual path. Ultimately, all of us by our aspiration, our dedicated practice, and our willed opening to the spirit, can bring into being this larger, extraordinary life, and correspondingly, a larger earth.

Steven Michael Matias

Steven Matias has been a student of Paul Dong's for several years. He is a body work teacher and therapist, as well as a researcher and writer, and his involvement with Eastern philosophy spans more than 30 years.

# Glossary

**acupuncture** (*zhen jiu*)   An ancient Chinese medical technique involving the placement of needles in the acupuncture points to adjust the flow of chi and restore the body's balance. This practice, a standard part of Chinese medicine, has now been recognized and legitimized in many countries around the world.

**acupuncture points** (*xue wei*)   Key positions on the meridians directing the transmission of energy and information through the body. Chinese medicine has defined hundreds of acupuncture points on the body and identified their relations to other body parts and their medical applications.

*chi* (also spelled *qi*)   An intangible and invisible "subtle energy" flowing through the body and having a close relation to physical and spiritual health. It is believed to be some kind of energy and information flow. Scientists have attempted to associate it with various types of radiation and magnetism in an attempt to measure chi, but its physical basis is still a mystery awaiting further research.

*chi kung* (also spelled *chi gong* or *qi gong*)   An ancient Chinese practice for cultivation of the mind, body, and spirit through meditation for emptying, relaxing, and quieting the mind to let the chi flow freely. This practice can lead to stronger chi for martial arts or healing purposes.

**circuits** (*zhou qi*)   Pathways of the circulation of chi from the dan tian point, around the body, and back again. Opening the circuits is an important part of chi kung.

*dan tian* **point**   An acupuncture point slightly below the navel, considered to be the central storage point of the body's chi.

**empty force martial arts** (*ling kong jing*)   A powerful martial arts technique which focuses the body's energy and projects it instantly to defeat an opponent without physical contact.

**external chi** (*wai chi*)   Chi projected outside of the body to affect other objects or people. It can be used for healing or for martial arts.

**horse trot** (*ma bu zhan zhuang*)   Another name for standing-on-stake.

**intention** (*yi*)   An expression of the mind's choices. Intention is a link between the subjective world and physical reality, and it plays an important role in mind-body practices for healing or martial arts.

**intention fist** (*yi quan*)   A combination of martial arts and chi kung, with an emphasis on mind power. It involves physical contact, so in the strict sense it is not an empty force practice, but because it trains the mind power and develops the chi, it can form part of a practice leading to the empty force.

*jing* (**essence**)   The basic physical material making up the human body.

*jing* (**force**)   The explosive power of all the body's energy concentrated in a single point at a single moment. This is the source of the empty force.

*kong jing* (**empty force**)   Jing or explosive power producing an effect on other people or objects without physical contact.

**meridians** (*jing luo*) (also called **channels**)   Pathways of the movement of chi through the body. In Chinese medicine, they are believed to link all parts of the body together and regulate their functioning.

**mind** (*xin*)   The manifestation of the intention for guiding and controlling the body. Mind power is an important concept for the empty force.

**one-finger art** (*yi zhi chan*)   A technique for concentrating all the body's power in the index finger, usually for martial arts.

**pushing the air to attack a person** (*kong chi da ren*)   Another expression for empty force martial arts. However, the implication of this name may not be correct, because chi kung researchers believe that chi is much more than "air."

**relaxation** (*song*)   The freeing of the body and mind from pressures and worries to allow the natural processes to take over.

*shi jing* (**solid force**)   Jing or explosive power producing an effect on an object or person by physical contact.

**silent sitting** (*jing zuo*) A meditation technique involving sitting, relaxing, and clearing the mind to cultivate the chi.

**spirit** (*shen*) A higher level of consciousness guiding the mind and the intention.

**standing-on-stake** (*zhan zhuang*) A meditation technique involving standing with the legs slightly bent and the arms sticking out. This is the key practice for the empty force.

**stopping a sparrow in the palm** (*zhang zhong ting que*) A technique in which a chi kung or martial arts master holds a bird in the palm and the bird is unable to fly away.

**sword fingers** (*jian zhi*) A technique in which the index and middle fingers are joined together in a pointing position to send the internal energy.

*tai chi chuan* (also spelled *taiji quan*) A traditional Chinese practice involving rhythmic, graceful, and harmonious movements. It can be used for health promotion or martial arts.

**touching acupuncture points through the air** (*ge kong dian xue*) The use of external chi directed at a patient's acupuncture points for healing without physical contact.

**unity of Heaven and man** (*tian ren he yi*) A spiritual concept in which the practitioner submerges the ego and feels at one with the natural world.

**Wang, Xiangzhai** A famous empty force master. He developed the practice of intention fists.

**Wuji (boundless) style chi kung** (*wuji shi chi kung*) A chi kung practice involving the combination of mind power and physical power, strengthening the chi and potentially adding it to the jing. This can give rise to the empty force.

**Yang, Luchan** A famous empty force master. He developed a practice combining standing-on-stake and tai chi.

*yi quan* See **intention fist**.

**yin-yang principle** A Chinese philosophical tradition which holds that the universe consists of interdependent and counterbalancing negative (yin) and positive (yang) elements.

**Yue, Huanzhi** (sometimes spelled **Le Wan Zhi**)   A famous empty force master. He attained the power by combining tai chi practice with Tibetan esoteric Buddhism.

# Bibliography

Paul Andersen, *The Method of Holding the Three Ones*, London: Curzon Press Ltd., 1980.

Richard Bertschinger, *The Secret of Everlasting Life*, Shaftesbury: Element Books Ltd., 1994.

Joseph Campbell and Charles Muses, *In All Her Names*, San Francisco: Harper Collins Publishers, Inc., 1992.

Mantak Chia and Maneewhan Chia. *Bone Marrow Nei Kung*. Huntington, NY: Healing Tao Press, 1989.

Lam Kam Chuen, *The Way of Energy*, New York: Simon and Schuster, 1991.

Paul Crompton, *The Art of Tai Chi*, Shaftesbury: Element Books Ltd., 1993.

Paul Crompton, *The Elements of Tai Chi*, Shaftesbury: Element Books Ltd., 1990.

Jan Diepersloot, *Warriors of Stillness*, Walnut Creek, CA.: Center for Healing & the Arts, 1995.

Paul Dong and Aristide Esser, *Chi Gong: The Ancient Chinese Way to Health*, New York: Paragon House, 1990.

Jane Hallander, "Chinese Empty Force" in *Karate/Kung Fu Illustrated*, May 1986, pps. 32–36.

——, "Look Ma . . . No Hands" in *Martial Arts Masters*, May 1993, pps. 68–71.

Jane Huang, *The Primordial Breath*, Vol. I. Torrance, CA.: Original Books Inc., 1987.

——, *The Primordial Breath*, Vol. II. Torrance, CA.: Original Books Inc., 1990.

Dr. Yang Jwing-Ming, *Muscle/Tendon Changing and Marrow/Brain Washing Chi Kung*, Jamaica Plain, Mass.: YMAA Publication Center, 1989.

Wong Kiew Kit, *The Art of Chi Kung*, Shaftesbury: Element Books Ltd., 1993.

James MacRitchie, *Health Essentials: Chi Kung*, Shaftesbury: Element Books Ltd., 1993.

Michael Murphy, *The Future of the Body*, Los Angeles: Jeremy P. Tarcher Inc., 1992.

Joseph Needham, *Science and Civilization in China*, Cambridge, U.K.: University Press, 1983.

Fang Nelli and Cai Song Fang, *Wujishi Breathing Exercise*, Hong Kong: Medicine and Health Pub. Co., 1986.

Stuart Olson, *The Jade Emperor's Mind Seal Classic*, St. Paul: Dragon Door Pub., Inc., 1992.

Chang Po-Tuan, *Understanding Reality*, Honolulu: University of Hawaii Press, 1987.

Richard Wilhelm (trans.), *The Secret of the Golden Flower*, London: Routledge and Kegan Paul, 1931.

Tom Williams, *Health Essentials: Chinese Medicine*, Shaftesbury: Element Books Ltd., 1995.

Doc Fai Wong and Jane Hallander, *Tai Chi Chuan's Internal Secrets*, Burbank: Unique Pub., Inc., 1991.

Wang Xuanjie, *Da Cheng Quan*, Hong Kong: Hai Feng Pub. Co. Ltd., 1988.

Lu K'uan Yu, *Taoist Yoga: Alchemy and Immortality*, New York: Samuel Weiser Inc., 1970.

# Index